How
ALMIGHTY GOD
Can Use a
SIMPLE GUY

STANLEY RIDLEN

ISBN 979-8-89485-351-2 (Paperback)
ISBN 979-8-89485-352-9 (Digital)

Covenant Books
11661 Hwy 707
Murrells Inlet, SC 29576
www.covenantbooks.com

To Rhonda. Thanks for letting God use you as part of my healing.
To my children and grandchildren. To explain
my love for you, there are no words.

Introduction

Over the last year and a half or two, the Lord has been leading me to share my stories, which in themselves don't account for much. However, when I look at what the Lord has done, the stories are rich with His hand moving in different areas throughout my life, and His fingerprints are all over anything good that has come of me.

Growing up, Mom and Dad always kept us in church, for which I'm very grateful. I won't pretend that I was always delighted to go the many times they made me, but as I look back, I'm fortunate and blessed to have parents who taught me the importance of spiritual life. I have many memories, good and not so good, from the folks who attended and led the church we attended. Carving out a way of understanding the difference between church and spiritual life, I thank Jesus Christ for showing me the unmistakable difference. I highly encourage anyone reading this to learn the difference, pray, and ask in Jesus's name for clarity—He is waiting to give (James 1:5).

Two mentors during our time in Marion, Indiana (2015–2021), greatly impacted my life for the Lord. One has been very encouraging to me personally, and he has continued to follow up with me even though we have not seen each other for approximately five years. He is a great accountability partner and has completely changed my life for God's glory and my own good in true humility and self-discipline. The other mentor led a Bible study that I was in while in Marion for approximately two years. In confiding in this mentor, he confronted me and my weaknesses in unique ways for the glory of God's kingdom. One example of this was when, in sharing with him my weakness of difficulty speaking out about what the Lord has done for me, he asked me a question instead of giving me advice, as Jesus does so many times in Scripture. That question was, "Has God done anything for you?" Those words stuck with me for many months as I continued to grapple with that question. This work will be filled with stories that attempt to answer that question.

To begin this work and to end this work, I will attempt to answer a similar but different question. A question that many people have asked me over the years and months of our mission work. That question is this: "How can I know that I am saved?" This question is also one that I've grappled with over months, and I find that many other Christians do as well. I will toss a few ideas out at the beginning of this work, but I intend to be a little more detailed at the end. I'm not a seminary graduate or some type of theologian, but I am a simple man, and God has moved me in many ways, giving me some real answers to the two previous questions. While I've joked with some friends about these stories being mine and that they can't have them, I'm quick to say that God is waiting to give them their own stories.

These stories that I'll share will not be in exact chronological order, as some overlap, and they will include things from my childhood. The focus will be on events after the age of fifty-six. Having been a believer in Jesus Christ since I was seventeen, much of my adult life was spent attempting to convince God that my way was best. For many of those years, I gave God most of the areas of my life, but that's not what He commands.

I must admit I resisted due to false humility and pride, but the Lord brought me to this place where the stories are no longer mine but His. While the stories in this work are very personal to me, I sincerely believe that others can benefit from pieces of these stories applied to their own lives when driven by God.

Early in my life, we lived on the north side of Kokomo, Indiana—Mom, Dad, my brother, and I, along with the little black dog. At about four years old, we moved to a home on the far north side of Kokomo, into a house I'll never forget. It was a newer home in a newer neighborhood with lots of children and lots of new friends. We hadn't been at the home long; as I recall, when I was four or five years old, my dad received a cigarette lighter from my uncle as a gift. Dad never smoked, but he made sure to show me where he kept this lighter and to never touch it or play with it. Anyone who knows me very well knows where this is going already.

Back in the days when we could walk the streets without much concern regarding safety, my dad gave me a dollar to go buy some candy at a downtown drugstore. Imagine that—a dollar. Well, with fifteen cents, I filled my pockets and was on my way back to give the eighty-five cents back to my dad, whom I had learned worked very hard for the money to support our family. On the way to a secluded area of downtown, four boys on bicycles surrounded me and ordered me to give them the money. I was ready to go to my death for those eighty-five cents. Just as things were heating up, a police car went by, and the officer shouted out the window of his squad car, "Is everything alright, guys?"

Four guys yelled "Yes," and of course I yelled "No!"

Before the guys on bikes knew what was going on, I ran as fast as I could back to my grandpa's house and arrived there safely. I have been fond of police officers ever since, and this story may be part of the godly example they laid out before us. I remember they always had a moment to answer questions and look us in the eye. They taught us by example how to respect our grandmothers, siblings, cousins, and all members of the family.

I remember watching as my father and grandfather dug a hole in the backyard of my grandpa's house to fix a plumbing problem underground. I was just a little guy, and it looked like that hole they were digging reached all the way to China. Being just a little guy, the men were concerned I might fall into the hole. They continually reminded me to stay back, which I reluctantly complied with. When they got the hole completed, I remember Grandpa was almost over his head in the hole. He and Dad then invited me down into the hole with Grandpa to allow me to see their handiwork.

The fact that they included me in their project always stuck with me—not simply telling me I was important but showing me I was. My maternal grandfather showed me some of the workings of the farm and taught me what it was like to ride in the bucket of a tractor that must have reached fifty feet into the air. At least it seemed like it was that high to the little guy that I was. Later in life, Grandpa had to move into town from the rural farm because it became too much for him to handle. My brother jumped right in to help, and I followed. Grandpa and Grandma were most grateful for the assistance, though being family, what we were doing to help didn't seem like much.

So Dad was at work, Dan was at school, and Mom was playing the piano in the living room. I touched the lighter. It wasn't long before the whole back of the house was on fire. I ran out to Mom, unable to speak, and the next thing I knew, there were at least one thousand fire trucks in front of the house. I just knew that if I didn't die in the fire, my parents were going to kill me. The firefighters and police officers were very kind. Mom and Dad were way more understanding than they could have been. They always found a way to love me and forgive me, even though I couldn't yet understand it. I can't guess how many times that story has been told at family gatherings and passed down through the generations. Many laughs have been had, but it wasn't very funny at the time.

Grandpa and Grandma Ridlen had rental properties on the same block where they lived in downtown Kokomo. One of the rentals happened to be open at the time, and Mom, Dad, my brother, and I moved into that home until the repairs were completed on the north side house. It seemed like forever, and I got a lot of reminders about what I had done, mainly from waking up each morning in a strange house.

Eventually, after we moved back into the home in northern Kokomo and got settled in, we went to school. We attended Bon Air School from first grade through eighth grade. During these early years, we had many football games in the backyard, baseball games where we'd break out a neighbor's window with the home run ball, and track meets in the backyard where we built standards for a pole vault pit that consisted of a couple of mattresses and homemade stair rails to use as pole vault poles. We found a rock that was perfect to use as a shot put. Many neighborhood kids would come over and bring their friends or family, and before long, we had a north enders versus south enders football competition regularly in the schoolyard.

As the competition grew, we would ride our bicycles to the south end of the designated area and, of course, challenge the south enders on their own turf. Many chipped teeth, bumps, and bruises later, strong relationships were formed, and healthy competition—sometimes not-so-healthy competition. These sandlot competitions were in addition to the school basketball, football games, and track meets. So there was a new school built in the south end of town where children from the perimeter of town would attend. In other words, we attended the southwestern school from the far north end of Kokomo. It was called Haworth High School. This new redistricting concept was certainly figured out by someone much smarter than me (well, maybe not too much smarter). I'm thankful for the way it was redistricted. We got to team up with many of the competitors from the sandlot experiences, and some very good football, basketball, and track teams were the result. Some good memories came from that school.

My brother was able to take his backyard pole vault lessons and turn them into a state championship medal. He also gained national recognition for the event, and with Mom, Dad, and I, we traveled west to California, Colorado, and some other area track meets. He continued his winning ways in the Big Ten, obtaining a full-ride scholarship to Indiana University. Since I couldn't run—certainly couldn't run carrying a pole—the pole vault event was not for me. I really enjoyed the events in track, particularly the relays and, of course, the pole vault. Having a different skill set and a bit of a temper, I decided to throw things, namely the shot put and discus.

There were a lot of other great athletes on the track team, and we had state recognition from many of them. I ended up attending a two-year school in Jackson, Michigan, on a track scholarship and added the javelin throw to my resume. Coach Red and Coach Blue (we will call them), along with other assistant track coaches and weight room coaches, made a major impact on my life. We spent many hours in the weight room with other athletes and coaches. Coach Red and I had a very close relationship that I will never forget. It started in the football locker room where I was a manager handing out equipment. One day, Coach asked why I didn't play football. I responded that I would love to, but there was no way I could. He advised me that I could play football if I wanted to, but it would take some hard work. The coach invited me to the weight room after school on any weekday, and he would guide me on how to get ready. I accepted Coach's offer, and it wasn't long before we were meeting on weekends in the weight room as well. We put in many hours in the weight room, particularly over holiday breaks. I gained a lot of strength over several months in the weight room and ended up joining the football team. I wasn't much of a football player, but Coach Red and the other coaches were very patient and allowed me to snap the long ball for punts and extra points. This way, I was able to earn a third letter and the coveted letter jacket.

I really enjoyed throwing the shot put and discus and was able to attend the state track meet in Indianapolis in both events. I was seeded second in the state of Indiana going into the end-of-year tournament. I told Coach (jokingly, of course) that I was sure the first-place guy had lied about his stats to become first. I felt a lot of pressure to win the state in the discus as, of course, my brother had won the state in the pole vault. That didn't work out so well, as anyone who's an athlete understands high stress, especially self-inflicted, can be devastating. I placed fifth in the state, and the officials mistakenly awarded me the fourth-place medal. Full disclosure: I did take a minute to contemplate keeping the fourth-place medal. However, I did return it to its rightful owner and accepted my fifth-place award. I looked up the athlete who earned fourth place, and we corrected the problem and had a little laugh out of the deal.

My brother and I ribbed each other a little bit about our capabilities. I particularly enjoyed reminding him that I was a two-event athlete, and while he was winning points for the pole vault, I was winning twice as many points for the shot put and discus. It never ended well for me, as I was often reminded of his state championship. Couldn't top that one, of course. We had fun with it.

There are so many great memories of high school and college sports. I continue to be thankful to God for some of the talents that He gave me. Many friendships have been enjoyed through the church and schools we've been involved in. I always had a love for baseball, especially Little League. I played for three years with three different sponsored teams. The last year I played, our team won the coveted city championship.

Some close friends at our current Bible study were involved in the team and/or have memories of this time together. Occasionally, we discuss different things that happened during that time frame. Many years have changed all of us, but the ones I speak of have been changed by Jesus Christ, as have I. Another favorite memory from baseball is when the new league for sixteen- to eighteen-year-olds was formed in town. Many of these were fine Christian men who had an impact on my life, and I'm so grateful for them. You see, there's way more to this than hitting a baseball or throwing a discus. Many life lessons were learned in how to behave, how not to behave, integrity, etc.

Coach Red took a particular interest in me outside of school as well. During summer break in the early 1970s, the coach was building a home for his family. He invited me over many times to have a meal and just talk. One of the things I'll never forget that he did was invite me to work with him in building his house, and he taught me how to roof. It put a little money in my pocket at the time, but little did I know that many years later, I would use that skill on a construction crew that I worked with. I'll always be grateful for Coach Red and how he impacted my life.

In April 1977, I was married for the first time. It was a very difficult year as I attended the Indiana State Police Academy in Plainfield. Four months of training and only being able to come home on weekends is not recommended so early in a marriage. God was ever-present with us through many difficult times. One example of how God showed up in a very surprising way involved the birth of our first-born son.

During the time of our transition to employment at the Kokomo Police Department, on June 30, 1977, our son blessed our family with his arrival four days earlier, on June 26, 1977. It was one of the best days of my life (and still is). His arrival put us in a difficult situation as we had to move to Kokomo for swearing in, and not being employed (technically) at the time of his birth, insurance coverage was not available. Our new baby had some health problems at birth and was in the intensive care unit for several days. The bills stacked up quickly. As a new police officer in town, I wasn't well-connected with folks yet. I was called and advised to show up at an attorney's office. Not being told why, I was very nervous. I had no secrets that would prevent me from being hired. What could it be?

When I entered the attorney's office, he invited me to sit down. I was told this would be a very short meeting as he handed me his business card. The attorney said he had heard that we had a baby born four days before my swearing in and that I was concerned about the bills. Of course, I said yes, I am concerned. He said, "You have my card. If any doctors or hospitals call you, just give them my information and have them contact me." I never received a phone call or a medical bill from the time of that meeting. What a great God we serve! I didn't see that one coming (Exodus 14:14).

After a couple of years of college, hard work as an athlete, and several temporary jobs, it seemed time to settle down and start my adult life. I was very interested in becoming a police officer and completed a couple of years of college toward that end. I applied to the Kokomo Police Department as well as the Indiana State Police. Following many background checks, physical ability exams, and psychological exams, the Indiana State Police is where I went to work. Prior to reporting in September of 1977, I got married in April of 1977. This was a highly stressful time for my new wife and me, but I was convinced that I could conquer the world. Reporting to the state police academy from September to December of 1977, the recruits and I lived at the academy from Sunday nights to Friday evenings. Not an ideal schedule for a newly married couple, to say the least. Upon graduation on a Friday in December, we were required to report to our new duty station on Sunday, two days later. That made Saturday *move day*. My wife and I moved from Kokomo to the east side of Indianapolis on Saturday. The stress was overwhelming. I was assigned to drive to my training officer's residence and start duty Sunday at 6:00 a.m. I laid awake all night knowing that my first day of work would include catching a bank robber, a murderer, and being shot at. It must have been 5:00 a.m. before I went to sleep, and as you can imagine, I did not make it to my training officer's residence on time. My new mentor and I settled in after a few good laughs, and he was very generous and kind in his evaluation. It didn't take much longer than a week of being on duty in Indianapolis before I was shot at by a bad guy. Fortunately, it was a low-percentage shot that missed the mark, but the event had a major impact on my mental and emotional health. Early on in my career, I realized there were situations that I did not want to see or experience. Running away shouting, "Somebody call the police," is not an option when you are the police.

In November of 1978, a horrible crime was committed in Speedway, Indiana. At a Burger Chef restaurant at closing time on a Friday night, four young people were closing the store. Robbers entered the back door and kidnapped the four young people. They were driven to a field in a wooded area in Johnson County, several miles south of where the crime began. No doubt the employees didn't show up for work on Friday knowing they wouldn't be going home again. I came to work on Sunday in Johnson County and learned that the bodies had just been located. Though I wasn't closely in contact with the crime scene investigation, I assisted with the perimeter on that Sunday. I attended many police debriefings and investigative meetings with Indiana State Police, Greenwood Police, Franklin Police, Speedway Police, and other departments. This crime had a major impact on my life and career at the very tender age of twenty-three. These are scenes and conversations that can't be removed and are very difficult to set aside and try to sleep at night. God is so faithful and present when we need Him most. He is so real (Psalm 23, 91)!

I learned a little bit during this investigation about the impact this crime had on four young people, their families, the community, many police officers, and myself. Looking back on all I was going through, it would have been wise to speak to someone about my struggles. During this time, life went on and many other events took place, but I didn't always deal with them in a healthy way. Jesus Christ was always with me, and I knew that, but I had a lot to figure out, including a very important question. I knew that He did; I just didn't know why He did or how He could love me as a simple, confused north-end boy. "Why did Jesus Christ care about me?" I became rather callous and self-sufficient, and many times numb from deep wounds that I wasn't sure how to deal with. I would get close to being free from the previously described wounds, and other serious things would happen that would open the old wounds and add new ones.

A few short years later, after starting my career at the Kokomo Police Department, I was working the midnight shift, never knowing when to be sleepy or hungry but knowing I always had to be the tough guy. At least that's what I thought. In the early morning hours of my shift, I was dispatched to a vehicle accident with injuries where a vehicle was turned on its side and another vehicle had run into a building. I arrived at one of the most spectacular scenes I've ever witnessed at a crash scene, where gasoline was leaking onto the street, a Kokomo natural gas line was leaking, and several people were injured. I never was an officer who enjoyed sightseeing where multiple injuries and damage were concerned. I remember wading through all the carnage, praying and thanking God that I could be there to help in any way that I could. In those moments, many times, training comes back to you automatically, as unfortunately, police officers have too many opportunities to witness. Almost immediately, many police officers arrived to assist. Fire trucks and ambulance crews arrived as well as the gas company, and the coroner was advised to be on the way. Many neighbors heard the crash and were guided away from the scene and away from danger. The fire trucks have so many bright lights on them that even though it was the middle of the night, it appeared to be the middle of the day. In the middle of the street, one of the vehicles involved in the accident, an older van, had flipped over on its side. The man we believed to be the driver had been decapitated during the crash. In those moments, with all the sights, smells, and emotions, I was deeply troubled.

The coroner arrived, a gentleman I liked as a person as well as a professional, and observed that the only way to identify the driver was to locate his wallet and driver's license. There was no one at the scene to be interviewed regarding the identity of the driver, as others were injured and taken to the hospital. As the van had tipped over on its side, the windshield was broken, and the coroner stepped inside the van through what used to be the windshield. The coroner was able to locate the driver's wallet. I watched over the coroner's shoulder as he exposed the driver's license. At this point, everything changed for me. It was like a dream, a bad dream. The world started spinning; it was as if it were daylight. We had more police officers than squad cars that shift, and I was doubled up (2 officers in the same squad car) with another officer. I went to my fellow officer and said, "Dave, get in the car."

He said, "What?" I did not know much of what I was doing, but I got behind the wheel, and Dave got in the passenger side door.

It did not take Dave long to see I was struggling, as he said, "Where are we going?"

I said, "I don't know." I knew the other accident investigators were coming or had already arrived to take measurements, and photographs, and take charge of this scene. To this day, I don't recall where I drove, but it wasn't far, as my fellow officer convinced me to pull over and let him drive. I don't recall much of what happened after he started driving. You see, the driver of the van was a friend from church that I had known almost my whole life. At some point, we ended up back at the crash scene, and the coroner asked me if I would like to go deliver the death notification to the family. This was not unusual for the coroner to include me or another officer in such an event. I knew I was in no shape to deliver such a message at that moment. So I thanked the coroner and declined the invitation.

This is another time it would have been good for me to get wise counsel, as I knew many pastors and believers who would give me support. As previously stated, life was happening very quickly as I had a young wife at home and one son who was eighteen months old. I talked with God often, but most of the time I didn't feel like He was there. A lot of things happened during these years that I did not understand. I mistakenly believed that I was the tough guy and could handle anything, but God loved me enough to show me that He was the one in charge and that I needed to trust Him. Dave was always a good friend after this event. He was very understanding of my not dealing with things in the acute emergency phase of this experience.

After being hired by the Kokomo Police Department in 1980, it didn't take me long to get oriented to the work, having been an Indiana State Trooper from 1977 to 1979. The Indiana State Police Academy was four weeks longer than the municipal and county academy. Most of what I needed to know I learned in the academy there, but learning how to fight crime on the streets was a new lesson for me. It was more than writing traffic tickets on the interstate.

I hired on with four other officers and having the academy under my belt, I went straight to a training officer to be trained on the street, while the others went to the academy for fourteen weeks. In my experience with the field training officer program at Kokomo PD, I would get four different training officers to educate me on Kokomo Police Department policies and procedures.

My first training officer was a roughneck. He had a hard shell with a very soft heart and was the perfect combination of rough and tough, and giving forgiveness. I'll never forget him because I started off from day one wanting to please him and had a healthy fear of him. On the first day of patrol with this Field training officer, he asked me, "What's your most important job working the street as a police officer?" I thought for a moment and got my tongue straightened out on this one.

After thinking through the question and the FTO demanding an answer, I told him, "My most important job as a police officer is to make sure I get safely to the end of my shift and make it home safely."

His reply was, "That's not the correct answer."

I really wanted to please my FTO, so as I nervously looked at him, he smiled and said, "Rookie, your most important job is to make sure I make it safely to the end of my shift and go home to my family." We both had a good laugh, though mine was rather a nervous one. It set the stage for our work together. He informed me that if we got in a fight while together, and if he got as much as a scratch on him, I'd better have my shirt torn off and be beaten up worse than him.

Not many days later, we got into a scuffle in the north end of town by some railroad tracks. As we pulled up to the scene, I witnessed a heavyset, middle-aged lady who had obviously been drinking. As we got out of the police vehicle, she recognized my FTO. She immediately started screaming in a rage, and it became obvious to me that she had had previous run-ins with the police. As the story goes, my training officer ordered her to quiet down and tell us what was going on. That did not happen, and the fight was on. I was in a spot as my memory went back to the previous conversation with my training officer. I jumped in, took charge, and boldly told my training officer I would take care of it.

As I wrestled with and handcuffed the intoxicated female, appropriately strapping her into the front seat of the squad car, I turned and nervously asked my field training officer if he was okay. He chuckled and said, "I'm fine, and so are you. Good job, rookie." From then on, working together, we understood each other quite well in that when things heated up, I would take care of things, and he could stand and watch and help if needed.

After being on the Kokomo Police Department for approximately a year, a group of officers got together, and our *quarterback*, who led the idea, started a fellowship of Christian police officers. This was a group of officers that met weekly for devotions, prayer, and to honor God together. Howard County sheriff's officers and other small-town deputies were invited to attend as well. It was interesting to watch God work through police officers who loved Him, and this fellowship grew and lasted many years.

After a year and a half or so, the officer that I called our quarterback above had another good idea. He gathered a group of officers and created a gospel-singing quartet, and we called ourselves the Peacemakers. We weren't really singers, but we were a group of Christian police officers who wanted to honor God. I was very blessed to be a part of this quartet, singing, playing the bass guitar, and testifying to what God had done in my life. I'm completely humbled by what God did through the ministry of the fellowship of Christian police officers and the Peacemakers. God really used our stories as officers who were dependent upon Him, and our quarterback officer, who through the Lord's will, brought it all together.

Having moved to Kokomo from the Greenwood area, it wasn't long into 1982 when my grandpa fell ill. He and Grandma were still living in the home they had been in for years in downtown Kokomo. Grandma couldn't take care of herself, and with Grandpa getting the new diagnosis of colon cancer and needing help, my wife, oldest son, and I moved in with Grandma and Grandpa to take care of them and to help us out on rent. My wife did more of the caregiving work, as I was a policeman on the midnight shift and had to sleep some too. Our second-born son was born while we were in that house, so it was a stressful time, to say the least.

Grandpa passed away in November 1982, shortly after his eighty-third birthday. I had done some part-time work, including transport at a local funeral home up until Grandpa became very ill. Upon preparation for Grandpa's funeral, the funeral home that I had worked for asked me a question that I didn't thoroughly understand at the time. They asked me if I would like to drive my grandpa to the cemetery and help put him to rest. It didn't take me long to say yes, and I did some thinking about that question and what a nice gesture that was from the folks at the funeral home where I no longer worked.

So normal grieving was going on, and I was learning that even though you know death is coming, it's not always easy. I thought I was prepared, as Grandpa had been ill for several months prior to his death. The day of the funeral came, and I thought that one of the staff from the funeral home would ride up front with me in the coach, but that wasn't to be. The day was cloudy and rainy, and the sky had settled in, looking like it was going to rain forever. As I was driving in the rain, I thought about how blessed I was to be transporting my grandfather to his final resting place. I must admit I choked back a few tears during that drive.

If I lived to be one hundred, I would never forget what happened at the end of that ride to the cemetery. I was pleased that I had fought back the tears successfully as the family members followed the coach in their vehicles. Just as I was approaching the entrance to the cemetery, the clouds parted, the sun came out, and tears began to flow. And did they flow! Here was that rough, tough cop melted down to a bucket of spaghetti. I had to slow the coach down to a speed slower than I was already going for fear I was going to run over something. That day, at that moment, I felt the arms of my Savior holding me and loving me, an undeserving servant of His.

Now I know what a lot of people think about this story—calling it a coincidence or whatever else. I know that in that moment, God parted the clouds, and I believe He did it for me, and I will always believe He did it for me. He wouldn't have had to, but He knew how to soften my stubborn heart, and He knew just what I needed. I read in Scripture that He parted the seas with His mighty hand for a group of undeserving folks. Since then, I have believed that God loves me enough to do such things, and when I am aware or wonder if it was Him or just the way things work out, I strive to praise His holy name! You can call me crazy, but when I wonder if it's Him or not, I'm going to give Him the credit as if it were. This has changed my relationship with Jesus Christ. I read that He really likes my praise as well. (*Elohim Tehillim*—God of my praise.)

Having been in the Kokomo Police Department for a few years now, I had learned the availabilities of extra hours and part-time work to raise a family of four (at the time). There was my wife, our oldest boy, our second-born boy, who filled our lives with many blessings, and me, who was blessed up to that time and since that time in more ways than I can understand. One of the activities was extra patrols, designed to make the streets safer in higher traffic times. Another was working security for a private restaurant in Kokomo that was very popular at the time. On two occasions, I found myself in a situation where these two opportunities overlapped and set up a situation of corruption that we called double-dipping.

Just prior to double-dipping the first time, I realized there was an overlap and went to one of the supervisors who also worked in both situations. I expressed my concern to the supervisor about the double-dipping. I was completely surprised by his reaction. He stated, "Don't worry about it. It happens all the time, and we all do it." There was no other way to cover the shift that I would be vacating to undo this. I went ahead and worked two overlapping shifts, each overlapping by only one hour both times. I knew it was wrong when I did it, not being able to cover the shifts another way, but I did it anyway.

I'll never forget what happened on a Friday night, the second time I had overlapping shifts. One of the other supervisors called me into his office and asked me to close the door. This was unusual, as in this office, it was usually informal, light conversation-type meetings. This was a fine Christian man that everybody knew was a Christian—not because he was quick to tell everybody he was a Christian, but because he lived life in such a manner that it was quite evident. He simply said, "Stan, don't go to the restaurant for your shift tonight. Top supervisors plan to go there during your shift, arrest you, and walk you out of the restaurant in handcuffs." There are a lot of back-stories involved here, but one of the striking things to me was that this supervisor could have forfeited his position if it was found out that he had told me their plan.

I did not show up for my shift at the restaurant that night. I was still working the street for the extra hour assignment described above.

Not long after I did not show up at the restaurant, the dispatcher called me on the radio and told me to report upstairs to the administration on the second floor of the city building. Knowing what the meeting was about, I became very nervous originally, but soon handed the situation over to the Lord and asked Him to take glory for His name, even though I had done some things seriously wrong.

Upon arrival on the second floor, I entered the office, and the two high-ranking officials sort of teamed up against me, playing good cop, bad cop (not like I had never seen that before). As you can imagine, it was not a very friendly conversation. Some fear tactics were used, including the possibility of losing my job as a police officer, criminal charges, and ruining my reputation with my fellow officers.

In a fashion that can only be described as the hand of the Holy Spirit leading me during this dark time, I reported to the high-ranking officers that I would not fear them or the circumstances to come, but I would respect them as my supervisors and would try to continue doing so. I did plead for my job but expressed to them verbally that I would be okay if they took my job from me. I said this in such a calm manner that it even surprised me—I can't imagine what they were thinking. This is proof of the presence of the Holy Spirit in me.

They informed me that I would be suspended for thirty days, during which time they would consider my future with Kokomo PD. Things were close financially for my wife and me at the time, and I wasn't sure how we'd make it—I just knew we would. One of the interesting questions the investigators asked me was, "Do you know of anybody else on the Kokomo Police Department double-dipping in this manner?" The look on my face must have been one of astonishment. It was clear to me that they wanted to turn my coworkers against me by answering this. I have every reason to believe that everybody knew it was going on and that many were participating in it.

Though it was a yes-or-no question, I did not answer it with a yes or no. As kindly as I could muster, I said, "It would be very simple to find out since there are schedules for both places. One could simply lay one schedule down on top of the other and clearly see if this has ever been done."

As I will attempt to explain, rather than making a whole lot of enemies regarding this situation, I made a whole lot of friends. With this kind of corruption going on in our department (on my part), news traveled fast. I will never forget the reactions of other officers who met me at the bottom of the elevator upon my exit from the administration wing. Many ranking officers surrounded me, shook hands with me, and asked what I had said and what they had asked. It was clear to me that they were concerned that their names might have come up, being implicated in the same double-dipping scheme. I wasn't very interested in talking with anybody at the time, but I assured them that the only person I talked about was myself and the wrongs I had done. There was a general sense from the other officers that everything would be alright—a lot of people breathing a sigh of relief as I marched out of the city building to begin my suspension.

It was a long thirty days that month of December when I served out my suspension. The Lord's hand moved in every direction during this time for myself and my family. Being close to Christmas and with this story having shown up in the newspaper, things started happening, such as groceries showing up on our porch, gift cards coming through the mail, and even a furnace installed in our home that an anonymous source paid for. A longtime friend of mine called and asked if I'd like to work for him. I could be his handyman at his heating and cooling business, and he would pay me the salary that I lost while on suspension (*Jehovah Ezri*—God my helper).

While working for my friend at a well-known restaurant on the east side of town, where many times police officers would meet for coffee or a meal, we looked up and observed the two high-ranking officers who had placed me on suspension—deservedly so—and my friend said, "Why don't you buy their lunch?" I thought about it for a moment, then declined.

My friend said, "I dare you." So I said okay, called the waitress over, and asked her to bring me their check. The high-ranking officers saw it coming and stopped it.

I prayed a lot during this time, flirted with a bout of depression, and had many conversations with godly men that I knew. This story is evidence that God is with us and loves us all the time, even when we don't behave like Christians. He doesn't just bless us when we *deserve it*, because we can't *deserve it* or earn it. One day, shortly before returning to work and thanking God that the administration allowed me to keep my job, I went to the station to talk to the upper administration. I explained to them how grateful I was that they allowed me to keep my job. Further, I asked them if they would allow me to call the entire department to roll call to begin the afternoon shift on the day of their choice. The purpose of my proposed meeting would be to apologize to the department for my corrupt behavior and to ask for their forgiveness.

I'm not sure what I expected as a result, but I was quite shocked at the reception I got following that speech and upon returning to work. This too was an act of the Holy Spirit being present with me, as I wanted to be anywhere except in front of the department asking for forgiveness for what many were guilty of. Knowing this, I carefully selected my words to place the blame squarely on my shoulders, where it belonged, and not to try to divert attention to anyone else. That seemingly won a lot of friends and influenced a few people, to say the least (*El Roi*—God who sees me).

One evening, while I was working the 2:00 p.m. to 10:00 p.m. shift after my suspension, the dispatcher called my badge number (230) after I had completed some paperwork. They asked me to call dispatch. At that time, the dispatcher advised that the high-ranking administrator who had suspended me for my corrupt behavior had a close family member who was injured in a car crash, and the status of the family member was uncertain. This accident had to have occurred at eight or eight thirty in the evening, just a little while before I was off work. The first thing that came to mind was that I should stop by the hospital, which was right on my way home anyway, and check the status of the family member and offer my prayers to the family.

Everything within me was screaming, "Lord, this can't be a good idea. I'm sure the ranking officer doesn't really want to see me right now. Besides, being this high-ranking, many people who answer to him will be there sharing their concern." I bargained with the Lord about not going and tried to convince Him my idea was best. Well, we all know the Lord's ways are best, so I headed to the hospital, trying desperately to find more excuses not to go. I wandered through the dark halls that night, hoping to be stopped by a nurse or a staff member telling me visiting hours were over, but who's going to stop a police officer in uniform in the hospital?

So I found out what room number they were in at intensive care and proceeded to the door. The door was slightly cracked open, so I gently tapped on it, and I heard a "Come in." Much to my surprise, when I opened the door, the ranking officer and his wife were the only two people present. The ranking officer was quite surprised to see me, as was his wife, with whom I was acquainted as well. I asked if there was an update on the family member (knowing the family member but not going to name him), and they were still uncertain at that time. Not wanting to stay too long, I offered a prayer for the family who seemed very grateful, and I left the hospital.

I talked with the Lord a lot on the way home, thanking Him for encouraging me to do the right thing. If you know me, you know that was the Lord, as I did not want to do it. As I recall, that accident happened on a Friday evening. Monday, after reporting to work at 2:00 p.m., I received a call on the radio to meet at the administrator's office. Here came the nerves again, wondering what else I might have done wrong. Upon arrival at the office, the ranking officer thanked me for coming to the hospital to check on his family member. I assured him of my prayers. He said, "That was quite a thing you did after having been suspended." I stated to him that I'm aware of the importance of families—that's more important than anything that's happened here. He chuckled and said, "You also got me in trouble."

When I asked why, he said that as soon as I left the hospital, his wife said, "Wasn't that the officer that you suspended just recently?" He blushingly said yes, and she said, "Shame on you."

So, you see, when the Lord works, He really works. And He changes people. He might have changed the ranking officer, or his family member, but I promise you, He changed me (Mark 12:30–31).

There are things that happen in our lives—police officers, nurses, or first responders—that we just don't want to see. I'll never forget, if I live, assisting with an investigation where a small child was killed. I was a rough, tough guy, and the police training officer with the young officer riding with me that night. And investigating the cause of death of this little one, the rough, tough guy left the building. The blond three-year-old who was deceased looked identical to my three-year-old daughter at home. My mind began to do some weird things that were not very fun. It was one of those times when I wanted to run out the door and yell, "Somebody call the police!" But you can't when you are the police. A lot of things happen during those types of investigations. A person's beliefs become real, and sharing grief with families and other officers can be very difficult.

Approaching the halfway point in my police career, many officers began to think, *Do I want to complete twenty years here or find another career?* I prayed a lot about a change and discussed it with my wife. I had a friend, a male RN, whom I spoke with often when I was in the emergency room. Due to my interest, he encouraged me to attend nursing school, so I considered it and checked out the possibilities.

As my interest grew, the city of Kokomo introduced a program that would pay for a degree in any major selected by the city employee. I went to verify this information with the human resources department and found it to be correct. In 1986, I began attending classes part-time while working at the department. Over the next five years, I worked full-time at Kokomo Police Department and part-time at Indiana University of Kokomo School of Nursing. As the last couple of years of nursing school was nearly full-time, this approach is not recommended. God blessed me many times and in many ways through these years. It was very difficult on my wife and the three children we had at the time. We had our fourth by the time I graduated and our fifth shortly after that: Anthony (previously mentioned), Aaron, Audrey, Alexander, and Abram.

Many humorous things happened during the career move from police officer to emergency department RN. Working on the street as an officer from 6:00 a.m. to 2:00 p.m., I responded to a traffic accident with minor injuries. One family member, however, needed to go to the hospital for his minor injuries to be treated. I worked the accident at approximately 1:00 p.m. and got off work at 2:00 p.m. I showered, changed into my ER scrubs, and arrived at the emergency room at approximately 2:45 p.m. The family and their loved one were still in the emergency room receiving care. You can imagine the looks I received from the family members. I smiled at them and said, "I suppose you saw my twin brother out on the street prior to your arrival at the ER." I then corrected my story and told them of my upcoming career change, and we all had a good laugh.

Not long before leaving the department, I suppose it was late February or early March of 1992, I responded to an indecent exposure call at a grocery store. It was very cold and icy on the streets that morning, around 11:15 a.m., when I got the call. As I arrived, the way the car was situated made it obvious which vehicle I was looking for, and it was also obvious what was going on inside the vehicle. The young lad was very shocked when I knocked on the window of his vehicle. The people who called in the complaint were staying around to make sure I did my job. I removed the young lad from the driver's seat, placing handcuffs on him per policy, and put him in the front seat of the squad car. Since he was a juvenile, I advised dispatch that I would be en route to juvenile intake with the subject. I had been carrying a nursing book in the seat, and as I put it in the back seat, I told him, "Don't ask."

Here's the funny part. The juvenile intake center was a large two-story building with a carport. Next door to it, there was another large two-story building with a carport. These two buildings didn't look much alike, but as you can see where this is going, I pulled the juvenile and the squad car into the wrong building, the Seiberling Mansion. (Stay with me.) I got out of the squad car, came around, and opened the passenger door. Grabbing his right arm to assist him to his feet, we both learned we were standing on ice. For reasons you can imagine, his pants weren't fixed too tight, and they started to fall. Handcuffs were still in place. We did quite a dance to stay on our feet and obviously keep him covered. Once we were on our feet, still unaware that I had pulled into the wrong place, we walked up the steps to the front door. Noticing people inside was not new, I went to open the door, and a nice gentleman inside pointed to the sign that said "Closed for Lunch." Unwilling to admit my mistake, I walked the juvenile back to the car and said, "It looks like we'll have to visit the mansion another time."

As if I wasn't embarrassed enough, coming back down the stairs to get back in the squad car to drive next door to the juvenile intake facility, I glanced across the yard and saw my sergeant standing on the steps of the building where he had come to back me up. The sergeant was not amused, arms crossed and glaring at us. I drove next door, corrected the problem, took the juvenile inside, turned him over to the juvenile authorities, and, yes, on the way past the sergeant, I repeated my comment that we would have to tour the museum another time. Upon getting inside the juvenile facility, I turned to the young lad and said, "I'll never tell anyone what you did if you don't tell anyone what I did." I encouraged the young lad to stay out of trouble from now on and told him he would be alright. (Sometimes you just have to laugh.)

In the fall of 1991, I was working extra duty at a dance on Kokomo's south side. It was a Sunday night, and many folks were showing up for the party and dance. We continued throughout the evening to get information about the bad guys who could be attending from out of town. The longer the evening went on, the more information we got. There were people coming through town, making the trip from Chicago to Cincinnati to distribute drugs and cause havoc. The more information that came in, the darker it got. Many of these folks were carrying weapons and were ready for a fight.

I was one of three officers working in the security detail that night. We were outnumbered nearly two hundred to three, and I stationed myself on the balcony overlooking the dance floor and the partygoers. I was about to encounter a situation that redefined what fear is. Along with the out-of-towners, there were several local troublemakers that I was very familiar with. Looking down from the balcony, I was sure one of the local troublemakers whom I had arrested in the past was present. The area was very crowded, but I was able to see (we'll call him Tommy) approach one of my fellow officers from behind and shove him. A wave of bodies moved across the floor, and I wasted no time racing to my fellow officer's side. When I arrived where the officer had been, the wave had moved into another area, and I could not locate him.

Being surrounded by hostile partygoers, I began to wonder how this evening was going to turn out. Being unable to locate either of my backup officers, a fight broke out, and two males were rolling on the floor in combat at my feet. People were yelling all around me, music was playing loudly, and it was very dark. As I bent over to separate the two combatants, someone pushed me very hard from behind. As I fell over a pile of bodies, my head banged against the corner of a very large stereo speaker. I was not sure if I was knocked completely out, but if I was, it was not for long.

The chaos of the loud music stopped as someone had turned off the sound system. Many people were yelling, and I was not sure in which direction the biggest threat existed. I remember it being so dark I couldn't see anything, and through the chaos, it was so loud I couldn't hear anything. Then someone sprayed Mace into the pile of bodies, which included me. At this time, I couldn't see, hear, or breathe. I guess I never realized how sweet oxygen really is. I was rolled up in a ball trying to protect myself, and I remember thinking, *Tonight I'm going to die.*

My training from the past had automatically kicked in. I remember rolling onto my right side, covering my duty revolver, and thinking that a bad guy might shoot me with his weapon, but he's not going to shoot me with mine. You see, from fellow officers and angry discussions with bad guys, it was a special showing of disrespect if a police officer was stripped of his gun and shot with it, or such a threat was made to an officer by a bad guy. Now lying on the floor on my right side, I really felt that my kidneys were exposed and that a bad guy would have a free shot at one of them with a gun or a blade or whatever they might have. With these possibilities streaming through my head, it became very real to me that the time for oxygen had come. I was in a bad place.

Another training tip came to mind: Crawl in one direction until you find a wall, then follow the wall to a door. I couldn't see as much as an exit sign when I started to crawl. Coming to a wall and following it, as I got closer to a door, I was able to get some oxygen. There's never been a sweeter feeling. In all that was going on, most of which I was not aware, I reached an exit door, and police officers and first responders were coming in from every direction. What a sweet sight that was. Before I knew it, I was at the back of the ambulance, getting ready to be taken to the hospital. Between the assessment of the EMTs and paramedics and my own assessment, I determined that my injuries were not severe enough to be taken to the emergency room. In thinking through this situation at least one thousand times, it remains real to me that that night could have been the end.

I remember very distinctly at the height of the danger and fear that I faced, saying to God, "I know You, and I trust You, and I'm ready to go home." I believe I said those words out loud, but I'm not sure due to the deficit in all my senses.

God's words back to me were, "Not tonight, Stan the man. I still have work for you to do." I know this story sounds overdramatic, but I know the spiritual warfare going on that evening was powerful and evident. God showed me His love and protection that evening, and I'll never stop praising Him.

> This day has salvation come to this house.
> (Luke 19:9a)

This scripture came to mind—that in the physical sense, Jesus saved me, again.

God has worked all through my life and has brought glory to His name despite me on many occasions. While finishing my last few years of police work, God led me through some very significant times. Some very tough times. You see, when our lives need change and we completely give things over to God, there is pain involved. Completing four college degrees after barely surviving high school is nothing short of God's hand moving. There is much to be said about my finally giving it all to God and withholding nothing from Him, but it has been the best thing I have ever done. Properly stated, it is one of the best things God has ever done for me.

To tell the story of my walk with God in a metaphor, I liken this walk to be like God and me taking a walk through my house and giving it all to Him. But when we get to the back room, He says, "Open this door, and let's see what's in here."

I quickly replied, "No, that's my personal room. Come out here to the living room and dining room; that's what needs fixing."

God did what I asked and left that room alone per my request. After continuing to walk in my way and not His, things got very unbearable. Finally, when I got to the very bottom, so to speak, I invited God back into my house. This time I told Him I wanted Him to have it all. He asked, "What about that back room that's locked?"

I replied, "Master, could we start there, please?"

We walk together now, and He loves me as much as He ever has, and I just want to serve Him. For many years, I thought that if I gave it all to Jesus, I'd be doing without. I have found since then that I was doing without when I was withholding some from Him. Now I'm free!

Through all the hours of police work coupled with education, there are a few years during that time that are a complete blur. I knew that in my studies and changing careers at that very busy time in my life, God was building something in me. Step by step, He continued to show me His way, and I wasn't always good at yielding. As previously stated, with change comes pain. There was plenty of pain to go around in our family. Doing things my way led to a lot of things, most of them not good. My way led to a divorce, bankruptcy, the loss of two businesses including a family farm, and a lot of pain for my first wife, our five children, and myself. There was a long trail and many skeletons along the way.

God was quick to forgive me, though it's been a long way home. I hope my ex-wife forgives me, and I hope my children forgive me. Much could be said about divorce, who is responsible for what, and the like. Suffice it to say if anyone's solely to blame, it's me. And looking back on things, I believe I married the wrong girl. And that's not her fault—it's mine. I certainly thank God and my first wife for the five wonderful children God has blessed us with. It can't be understated, the pain and the wreck that we have been through. I praise God in heaven that this is not where the story ends. We are so blessed that our family has continued to grow physically, emotionally, and spiritually.

> Surely the arm of the Lord is not too short to
> save, nor is His ear too dull to hear. (Isaiah 59:1)

This has become one of my favorite verses.

In 1992, I passed the Indiana State Board of Nursing licensure exam. Soon after that, in June 1992, I resigned from the Kokomo

Police Department and went to work at Saint Joseph Hospital Emergency Room.

In going through all the education, the Lord really helped me. As previously stated, I attended a junior college in Jackson, Michigan, right out of high school, where I nearly completed my law enforcement degree, now known as criminal justice. After completing my associate degree in nursing, I was able to take my hours from criminal justice and complete an associate degree in general studies. Following this, the Lord led me to Indiana Wesleyan, where I completed a bachelor's degree in nursing in 1997 and a master of business administration in 2000.

I had prayerfully considered all this education at my age. God had a plan that was much bigger than mine—one I would not have understood if someone had told me what was going to happen. The MBA program was generally group work, and as it was drawing to a close, we had a master's thesis research project that we were responsible for, which seemed way over my head. A group of five people were discussing our thesis project. Most of the other participants were supervisory auto workers, and naturally, they leaned toward a thesis in that realm. My strong desire was to do something related to health care. Not having any idea what that might be, I prayed, asking for God's guidance.

Only a week or two into my prayers, a cohort of mine and I were at a district meeting. We worked for a correctional health-care company at the time, and the district meeting discussion was regarding the costs and usage of medications in the Indiana prison system. The costs were outrageous, and the company we worked for, on contract with the Indiana DOC, was determined to get something done about it. In speaking with my cohort, the task seemed impossible! My cohort was a technology guy, and almost immediately he built the skeleton of a clinical pathway for psychotropic medication administration. We met a couple of times and fine-tuned the clinical pathway. Now all we needed was my supervisor's approval, the Indiana medical director's approval, and a few more miracles.

We only had weeks, not months, to put the plan in place, get approvals, and present our ideas to the state and the contracting company. There is no explanation other than the Holy Spirit guiding me, and the results are the evidence. I had a very good supervisor who could see the benefit of our proposal and guided me when I asked. Getting written permission from the state medical director and my supervisor was impossible in the time frame given. I was able to catch the state of Indiana medical director in the hall alone (not a coincidence) and explained in detail what I was up to. He asked some very pointed questions regarding my idea and implementation that normally would have been overwhelming. Instead, I answered each of his questions appropriately and got his verbal approval to move forward. This is completely unheard of.

The company moved me from my current assignment to the Indiana State Prison in Michigan City for a period of six months. During those six months, meetings were held with all departments, including medical, psychiatry, nursing, and custody officers. It was just like God to answer a big problem that was way beyond my understanding. From October 1999 to March 2000, I implemented my clinical pathway and realized absolutely zero adverse reactions to changes in medication administration. In addition, we cut the cost of medications by one-third. Also, the number of offenders taking medications was cut by one-third. My cohort, the power of the Holy Spirit, and I changed things, and our medications were delivered to the Indiana Department of Correction in a much more efficient way.

This efficient method of medication administration was presented to the corporate contractor, the state of Indiana, and at a conference in St. Louis, Missouri, where several hundred professionals came to observe our research. Also, a monthly correctional health-care magazine and a worldwide research journal printed our story. Quite a stir for a guy who didn't receive his first associate degree until he was in his upper thirties, and a simple guy at that. Ten years after all of the above, my clinical pathway was still in use in one facility that I know of in Indiana, and a doctor who had moved to California called and asked if he could use my work. I joyfully advised him he was welcome to use it.

After the presentations noted above and my moving from my position at the Indiana State Prison, I spoke with the vice president of the contracting company with whom I worked. I showed him the data proving the success of the system and implementation. He mumbled something along the lines of, "Your data shows the system does not work." After a short discussion, it was clear to me that he wasn't interested in improving the care or saving the taxpayers' money. Later, I learned why. The health-care contractor was in the process of purchasing the pharmacy. Yes, they did not want the prices to go down because the contracting company would make good use of the high prices by purchasing the pharmacy. Despite corruption, God is still in control.

One of the difficult things related to the divorce was my arrest—being handcuffed and taken out of the church I had been attending. It was difficult to see what God was doing at that time. I personally knew the shift commander who ordered me arrested and the officer who reluctantly placed me in handcuffs. I encouraged him to continue to do his job and thanked him for his reluctance. Taken in on that Sunday morning, the drunk tank was full of seven offenders not including myself. Most of the other seven were unconscious, and the room didn't smell very good, to say the least. Determined that I was not going to miss out on church, I started to softly sing: "Amazing Grace," "How Sweet the Sound," "On a Hill Far Away Stood an Old Rugged Cross," and "Just as I Am without One Plea." One of the offenders woke up, and we had a little talk.

I'm not sure God changed him that day, but God surely changed me. I came through the door of the jail a bitter, nonforgiving, miserable man, and left a grateful, blessed man. He has continued to change me in so many ways, some of which you'll read in this work.

In May 2006, I began working at the Veterans Administration Hospital in Marion, Indiana. This proved to be a "God thing" on so many levels. I was a nurse manager on an inpatient unit and developed many friendships with staff and veterans. I thought I knew a lot about mental health care, but I learned so much more about serving veterans who had fought for our freedom in many ways. So many people were hurting in so many ways and needed Jesus Christ in their lives. From day one at the VA, I viewed it as a mission and not a job.

After working at the VA for a year and a half, a friend approached me with an odd question. More than a casual acquaintance, I had worked with Andrea in different settings. She knew my story—that

I had been divorced for three years and that I was trying to live for Jesus. Her question was simple. She asked if I was dating anyone. It didn't take me long to answer no, and then to add that I wasn't interested. You see, the story is that I had been talking to the Lord for some weeks about meeting a lady that I could have dinner with on Friday evenings who reminded me of Jesus. You see, a failed marriage was the end, as far as I was concerned. God hates divorce. How could He possibly bless a second marriage that I knew I didn't deserve anyway?

After answering no, Andrea didn't give up. After asking me if I was dating, she said, "Do you know Sandy from upstairs?"

My answer was plain: "Yes, I know Sandy from upstairs, and I know she's married, and I'm definitely not interested in dating her."

We both had a laugh, and she said, "No, no, no—I'm talking about Sandy's ex-sister-in-law." Her ex-sister-in-law was a fine Christian lady who had been divorced for about three years. You see, Andrea knew me well, Sandy knew me distantly, Sandy knew Rhonda well, and Andrea knew Rhonda distantly.

As Andrea continued to speak with me about this possibility, I had some nervous feelings. Only weeks after praying to God to bring a casual relationship with a lady who reminds me of Jesus, He showed up! Having worked with Sandy on some committees, we knew each other, so at Andrea's bidding, I went to Sandy's office. After talking to both ladies, they told their stories of how the Lord spoke to them about bringing us together. Then I became nervous. Immediately upon leaving Sandy's office, I couldn't concentrate on anything except our conversations. I prayed again for God's will and to make sure I knew what He wanted me to know.

Andrea got ahold of me and asked me to go to Sandy's office, as she had something for me. I nearly ran to her office and then had to act all cool when I got there. Sandy said that she had just talked to Rhonda, and she handed me a piece of paper with Rhonda's phone number on it. Now I was nervous. I asked Sandy if Rhonda was expecting me to call. Now I was at a new level of nervousness. Feeling like I was sixteen or seventeen years old and had never dated before, being cool was out the door. I started wondering what I was going to say. My knees were banging together, my hands were sweaty (somebody wrote a song). I waited a little longer and couldn't think of anything or anybody else, so I just called her.

I identified myself and asked if it was okay that I called her, knowing I didn't deserve such a relationship even as a friend. I asked if it was okay if we met for dinner soon. She replied yes. I told Rhonda that I had done my homework, and I knew where she lived, but I suggested that she come and meet me at a restaurant since she didn't know me yet. Later, I would learn that she liked the way I was protecting her before she even knew me.

Well, the grapevine was buzzing at work, to say the least. I didn't sleep well at night and wasn't concentrating on my job when I was at work. It seemed something special was going to happen. It was a Wednesday evening, December 12, 2007, when Rhonda and I met at a local restaurant. I was there what seemed like an hour early, holding my breath until she came walking through the door, knowing she would take one look at me and run off. Well, it didn't happen quite that way. She walked in the door, and I stood to greet her. What a beautiful, cute, and sweet lady had come to meet me this evening. I was so nervous. I asked the Lord to not let me blow it.

The conversation started very pleasantly with the usual question, "How many children do you have?" She said she had four children, and I advised her I had five.

To myself, I whispered a prayer, *God, how can this work?*

He said, "Trust Me," so I did.

Rhonda floored me with a silly question that we still laugh about today. It took me completely off guard. The question was, "Do you like auto racing?"

My brain started working, *Where is she going with this? What should I answer?*

The Holy Spirit grabbed me as if to say, "Tell the truth." Well, I don't particularly like auto racing, and she doesn't look like a race car girl to me. She giggled so sweetly when she knew she had me thinking. So I told the truth: "No, I don't like auto racing." That must have been the right answer; she agreed to go out with me the next week.

From the very beginning, Rhonda and I loved to laugh and have a good time. So I told her what a nice time I had, and since she had agreed to go out with me again next week, I would come by her house and pick her up. She seemed delighted. I know I was. Starting with the second date, we kept wanting to be around each other a little more than one evening per week. It became real to me that God had blessed me with a relationship with a darling lady who reminded me of Jesus in the way she talked and the way she acted. God made it very clear to me that I wanted to be around this lady for the rest of my life. Apparently, she felt the same way too, as when I proposed to her, she replied yes. When I proposed, I told her she might as well say yes because if she didn't, I would just keep asking. We have a funny little story in the way I proposed. We talk about it and laugh about it often, but, well, that's a story for another time.

One of the foundations we wanted to set for our marriage included the idea that "we are going to outgive God." Of course, we would not pretend that we could ever do that. We just wanted a mindset to give and give and give. One of the many things I love about her is that she is such a kindhearted, giving person. And the context of our statement is not limited to just giving money.

We stayed at this church for nine years, serving in many ways. We served separate terms on the board, co-led small groups, and led the praise team. I'm so thankful for that church, as I really grew spiritually there. We met a man who was a veteran through that church, and we had a unique relationship with him. We'll call him Marty. He was ninety-seven years old when we took over his care—physically, mentally, and spiritually, we cared for him. What an experience. Just one more time, we can't outgive God, as He blessed us far more than we blessed him.

Marty was in his upper nineties, blind, and deaf. He was able to carry on a limited conversation and had a great sense of humor. Considering all these challenges, he didn't complain much. His family all preceded him in death. We quickly became his family. There was another lady taking care of his finances until he asked us to take over that part of his care too. Some of our children were able to develop a relationship with him too, as on occasion they would go over to minister to him along with us.

It was a great few years taking care of Marty, and he passed away when he was ninety-nine years old. I'll never forget our pastor telling us that Marty accepted Christ. What a blessing it was teaching Marty to pray. He wasn't so sure about it, and we chuckled, and I said, "Just keep it simple." I remember the simple funeral he had—a graveside service with only a few people present, as most of his friends as well as family had gone on ahead.

In 2006, when I became a nurse manager at the VA in Marion, I was advised of a new challenge I would face supervising a few of the staff on an inpatient psychiatric floor. My supervisor informed me of one employee who liked to stir up trouble. We'll call her Kathy. Kathy was very loyal and took care of the veterans on the unit, but she had plenty of mental health issues of her own. One of the things she did not like was having a supervisor in general—especially any male supervisor. Being in a union environment, many times she would request to speak to her union steward, or she would just leave the unit and go to the union office, which was a violation of the contract.

I tried my hardest to gently guide her in the way I wanted things to be done, which included not calling people names, swearing at people, and causing havoc on the unit. Over several months, I continued to try my best to lead the unit in a professional manner, with the veterans' care as the top priority. Most of the staff were vocal about believing in our methods of supervision on the unit. Many of them came to me with complaints regarding Kathy and her lack of professionalism. Most of the time, she did good work and was very loyal to the veterans and other staff members, but many times, her focus would jump in the tracks, and she would yell out in inappropriate ways.

Many times, union stewards would come to me and apologize that they had to come and represent Kathy, as many times her issues were unreasonable. This is where the story changes from Stan's story to God's story. I began to pray to God regarding Kathy and for myself, attempting to find better ways to manage her. It became clear to me that she needed attention, and I had been in a tug of war with her; she was very difficult to deal with. As I prayed for what was best for her, the Lord brought me a plan to give her attention in reasonable doses.

Many times, Kathy would become upset at morning meetings and become loud and vocal, arguing about how upper management or even middle management, which included me, was handling certain problems. It was very disruptive, and the Lord spoke to me one morning after the report. In my prayers, I was asking God to show me what the underlying problems might have been and how I might be able to deal with them and help her. Kathy was a single mom and had one daughter and one son. They, too, had reported mental health issues of their own, and at this point, I wasn't sure how they wouldn't.

The Lord walked me through a new idea, proving once again it was His story, not mine. I decided to move forward with what I now believe was God's plan, and that was to meet with Kathy each morning after the report for two minutes. Of course, this would only be on mornings when we did not have an emergency on the unit. She would come into my office each morning, and after a while, she became more pleasant to deal with. We laid some ground rules before we started this method of communication, and it worked quite nicely.

Being a male supervisor of mainly female staff, whenever I was in a private meeting with female staff, I would have the female staff member sitting closer to the door than I was, with the door cracked. There was always an understanding that if things got uncomfortable for the female staff member, she could just get up and walk out, and we would meet at another time. Just being married to my new wife for a short time, I was very meticulous about including her in what was going on in every aspect of my job, particularly in dealing with Kathy.

Most times during these two-minute meetings, Kathy would bring up issues that were going on with her children. I would try to listen carefully and not give advice unless it was asked for, and it usually wasn't asked for. Her children were getting assistance with some of their issues, and we would walk through some of those in my office. Through the special attention that she was getting, a bond was established. Other staff members were aware, and it seemed they appreciated it. God's plan was in dealing with Kathy.

Some of the staff advised me that they were concerned for Kathy's well-being during off-duty hours, as they thought she might harm herself. After consulting with my wife, we agreed that I would give my phone number to Kathy to be used only in case of an emergency during off-duty hours. I made it very clear to Kathy that I would only answer a phone call from her if my wife was present with me, and she would always be on the line during any off-duty conversation. I hesitantly gave her my phone number, hoping that she would not overuse it, and she never did call until one Saturday night.

As I recall, on that Saturday night, the phone rang, and it was her number on my caller ID. My wife and I were just turning out the lights to go to sleep, and honestly, I did not want to answer the call. God moved in me to do so, and we took the call. Kathy was at the other end of the line, extremely hysterical and inconsolable. Much of what she was saying was not understandable. I was very tired, as we had worked around the house a lot that day, and we oversaw the praise team on Sunday mornings, which took a lot of energy to manage.

We asked Kathy if she would like us to come and pray with her. She said she would like that, so we got her address and advised her we would be on the way. It was quite a distance, so I suppose it was thirty minutes or so when we arrived. She invited the two of us to sit down in her living room, and we talked for a good little bit. We prayed with her and taught her how she could pray to God on her own if she desired. We talked about how special our relationship with God is and how it changes how we think and how we do things. I was never sure if our meeting meant much to her, but I was convinced that we did what God asked us to do.

Kathy continued to have problems, we continued our meetings, and we continued to pray for her. Many months later, she concocted a story to try to cause me grief in the workplace. We ended up in some union meetings where we had to negotiate behaviors we would both try to stick to. Nothing she brought up really stuck to the wall—it was just an annoyance, as all the players were used to dealing with her behavior. I thank God for showing me how to take a less selfish approach in dealing with a difficult personality, to say the least.

God really moved in bringing my wife, Rhonda, and me together. Consistent with our approach of "trying to outgive God," He continued to move in miraculous ways and to use each of us individually and together to bring glory to His name. We had been serving in the same church for about nine years, and Rhonda and I had been very busy doing church things and trying to bring glory to God in the process.

The Lord led me to talk to the pastor about my leading a prayer group one day each week at the church. I already had a key, as we were doing many things in the church, and I was more than a little surprised at the response I got to that question. I told him I recognized that he was at the church almost every day, including many evenings, and I volunteered to just come and have a prayer meeting.

A dear couple, very godly people close to us, agreed to host a cottage prayer meeting at their home one night a week. Shortly after, another couple joined us, so there were six people hungry for God, inviting Him to do with our lives what He would. We had regular prayer meetings for a year and a half or two. Toward the end of almost two years of praying together, we were seeing God's hand move and hearing from God in intimate ways. I remember asking God to hurt my heart for what hurts His. God loved me enough to do that, though I did not know what I was asking. God was drawing each of us closer to Himself, and His moving was palpable. The cottage prayer group was becoming as powerful as God wanted it to be.

One day, my wife was driving down one of the main streets in Marion, and she saw a little church with a "For Sale" sign in front of it. She and I talked about it a little bit and agreed that I would call the number on the sign. We knew there were probably some good reasons not to start another church there, as evidenced by the fact that one had just closed, and there were three others within a few blocks. We continued to pray for God to guide us, and then the message became clear that we should pursue buying the building. I went through a process of trying to convince God that this plan did not make sense. In my flesh, nothing about it made sense.

We continued to pray. Many times, I rode my motorcycle to the building we were considering purchasing and prayed. One day, I was feeling particularly holy, and I asked God to show me whom we needed to minister to. Immediately after asking God to show me, He did. As I was sitting on my motorcycle talking with God, a door from an apartment building across the street swung open. A person came dancing out of the door with a boombox playing loud music and continued to dance down the street, waving at passersby, many of whom were honking. The individual was dressed in a party dress, high heels, and heavy makeup, and a few cars stopped to have a little chat. After that chat, and as the vehicle moved on, the individual waved to me. The individual continued to raise the full-length party dress above the knees, much to the liking of passersby.

It should be noted that by the time this part of the show was over, I had determined that this was not a female but someone who used to be. We'll call his name Darrell. A large range of emotions went through me during this intimate conversation with God. Well, I wanted to ask God, "Is there anyone else You would have us minister to?" But God knows me, and He knows we sometimes have humorous conversations. What I did ask was, "God, how would You have me minister to him?" The Holy Spirit in me was very clear with His answer—not an audible voice, of course, but the Holy Spirit communicated to me that I was to love him.

"God, please teach me how," was my reply. This was not a small lesson God was teaching me, as I had many biases related to this type of person. Again, this is another example of God doing something in me that I could not create on my own. This drastic lesson brought the reality to me that God wanted us to do something, though I wasn't sure what or how. The *when* was clear, and it should be right now.

Not long before this very meaningful talk with God, He had led me in 2017 to retire in a year (2018). In our numerous prayer times, both with others and with God speaking to me, I was still having trouble making sense of how this was going to work. I remember asking, "God, I assume this means I won't be retiring in a year."

God fed me another dose of humor when His Holy Spirit grabbed me by the heart as if to say, "Who said anything about the retirement plan changing?"

I remember laughing and thinking, *God, I love You. I do not understand You, but I love You and I trust You.*

In conversations with our prayer partners at cottage prayer and with my wife, we decided to make a bid on the building. We developed a not-for-profit organization called Faithful Partners of Hope. In organizing, we needed a CEO, which I was honored to accept. The gravity of the situation—retiring in a year and purchasing a closed church building—was very heavy. I won't pretend that I was good at it, but through the prayers of my warrior friends, praying to an almighty God who was listening, we moved forward. There was a time when I considered not moving forward, and everyone would have understood and loved me just the same.

A final decision on the building purchase needed to be made. I went to the building for personal prayer once again, and the Holy Spirit grabbed my heart and said to me, "Stan, you either trust Me, or you don't." Through tears, I told Him that I do and to help my unbelief. The board of FPOH put in an offer on the building. It was a ridiculously low offer, but it was accepted because God was in charge and not me. I learned more each day how God guided us, and how things continued not to make sense to me, but watching God work and being on His team was so powerful.

The man in charge of the cottage prayer meeting had become my mentor. He asked, "Can we read a book together, *Fresh Wind, Fresh Fire*?" The author is very dynamic. He speaks a lot about prayer and living for Jesus in this book. My mentor stated he would like for us to go hear him preach in Brooklyn, New York. The church had three morning services on Sunday and two prayer services on Tuesday—one in the early afternoon and the other in the evening. My mentor and I agreed to arrive in Brooklyn on Saturday and stay through Tuesday evening, heading home on Wednesday to attend each service.

I've never been in a church where the Spirit was more alive— worshiping with the Brooklyn Tabernacle Choir, meeting with several people who loved Jesus Christ and wanted to live for Him, and hearing some of the best and simplest preaching about God's love for us. The most touching parts of the trip were on Saturday afternoon, upon arrival at the hotel. My mentor and I got on our knees before the Lord and had an amazing prayer time. We called out to God, we laughed, we cried, and looking back, I believe the Holy Spirit was preparing us for what was about to happen on Sunday, Monday, and Tuesday.

When my mentor and I arrived at the church on Sunday morning, we went plenty early, as we had heard seats go fast. When we arrived, a lovely couple approached us and asked if we had a prayer need today. My mentor looked at me to give me the opportunity to answer. I nearly cried at the question, as we were really seeking God and were walking on sod completely foreign to me. As briefly as I could, I shared with the couple about our mission in Marion, Indiana. The foyer was very crowded, but they joined hands in a circle with my mentor and me and shook the gates of heaven right there in the busy church.

They told us briefly about their prayer ministry at Brooklyn Tabernacle Church and requested we exchange phone numbers. We did so, and they asked permission to call in thirty days to see how we were doing. It was clear they believed God was going to answer our prayers and many others that they must have dealt with that day. They went on to explain that their prayer requests go on a card, and they pray for folks for thirty days.

So approximately thirty days after returning to central Indiana, I received a call from the couple that we met in Brooklyn, New York. What a welcome phone call it was. They were not rushed to get off the phone to call the next person or distracted in any way that would take away from the impact of their call. We spoke for a good while, updating them on our mission in Marion, which was moving forward thanks to God's work.

I want my prayers to have an impact like my new friends from New York. I have implemented this concept of praying for others first at the Hope Community Center and in all my personal prayer life and devotional life.

So for clarification, Faithful Partners of Hope was the name of the not-for-profit organization that God built. Hope Community Center was the name of the building that God opened for His glory. During our organization and in finding out who we are in Christ, we developed a ministry named "Call to the Streets" (more about programs later).

During this time, we would go out door to door in the neighborhood, or if we saw someone walking their dog or mowing their yard, and the Lord led us to speak to them, we would simply ask, "Do you need prayer today?"

I used prayer cards and made many follow-up calls in thirty days to see how people were doing. Another reminder to me that God is in charge is that many times I don't really want to do what He's asking. I would love to pretend that I'm always "right in the center of the will of God," but many times I have weaknesses and doubts, and the devil gets my ear sometimes. But God is so faithful, and He has taught me that even though my first nudge doesn't always get me moving, His faithfulness does.

God loves me so much and has never given up on me, and thank God, He's never given me what I deserve. I've been so blessed in working with the Lord, and He has blessed me with many stories to pass along. In all the folks I've dealt with in this ministry and others that I'm a part of, a burning question continues to come up. That question is, "How do I know that I'm saved?" The stories above and the ones to follow are very powerful; some might make you laugh; some might make you cry, but they're stories about what God has done in a regular, simple North End boy who just decided to say yes.

Please read my stories and know that you can't have them, as they're mine. But God is just waiting to write your stories with you—just give it all to Him and hold on. Another mentor of mine helped me answer the question, "How do I know that I'm saved?" A long talk ensued. I shared with him the fact that I was not good at sharing what God had done for me. As Jesus did on many occasions, he didn't give answers; he asked questions. This mentor asked, "Has God ever done anything for you, Stan?"

I tearfully answered, and we talked about me not giving my all but wanting to hold certain parts of my life for myself. My mentor further explained, "When you come to Jesus, get ready to die." We talked about how many people believe that they get saved and think their problems are all gone. Then he walked me through what baptism and communion really mean. Short story—we die with Him so that we may live with Him.

So it was June 2017. We had been part of a cottage prayer group for a year and a half or so. We had been praying for God's direction for what ministry He would have us lead, and He led us to a building that would soon become a community center. We closed the contract on the property. My wife and I went to clean up the property, plant some flowers, pick up some trash, and the like. It was a beautiful day, and many people were walking by, some driving by, and some people stopped to ask what we were doing.

"Is it going to be a church?" one man asked.

I pointed south and said, "See that church down the street?" Then I pointed to the north and said, "See those two churches down there?" He said yes. I said, "I don't believe we need another church on this block, do you?" It was interesting, the questions that we received without answers. I found that was exactly where my life was. The Lord was saying buy the building, and we did that, but we didn't know the next steps.

Very quickly, the board of directors agreed to move our weekly prayer meeting to our new place. During the warm months, we would have prayer meetings outside in the parking lot. We would bring folding chairs from inside the building, put them in the parking lot, and we always left one vacant for the next person who wanted to join. Before long, some people from the neighborhood would join us for prayer. Some would come very regularly, and some occasionally. It was a safe place where we knew God was doing something, though for a period, we weren't sure what that was.

We had agreed from the start to always ask God what His plans were and to help us understand them. It kind of felt like the story of Noah building an ark before there were any rain clouds. We continued to pray and ended up with what we called a community center named Hope Community Center. My daughter and her husband and daughter were moving from Kokomo to Rochester with his work. They had two pianos, so they ended up loaning one to us during the move. Many times during prayer meetings, someone would play the piano, and we would sing praises to God. We got a lot of use out of that piano, and it was great the way God worked that out.

As the Lord led, we would have meetings with Bible teaching, testimony time, or a music special. At the community center, we had some fundraisers and many volunteers who helped us out by reaching out to the community. One Saturday, there was a cookout with lots of great food. We invited nursing students from Indiana Wesleyan University to check people's blood pressure and educate them on healthy living habits. Interest and excitement grew for what the Lord was doing at Hope Community Center.

Three young guys from the VA hospital in Marion, whom my wife and I were familiar with, came and assisted in serving people. They all made it clear after that cookout that they wanted to be involved as volunteers at Hope. They volunteered to help with some projects, such as painting around the building.

One weekend, we had a workday on Saturday. The floor inside the building needed attention as it was a wooden, scratched-up floor. Some of the painting that needed to be done was fifteen to twenty feet in the air, and I wasn't sure how we were going to get that done. On that Saturday morning, our list of chores was very great, but the workers were few.

One of the members of the board needed to stop by the mission building in Marion. I don't recall why he was there except to be used by God. While he was at the mission, a group of adults with a youth group from a church somewhere in Pennsylvania entered the mission. Our board member heard the leader of the youth group tell this story to the mission staff. A group of teenagers had come from Pennsylvania to an event at Indiana Wesleyan University (about one and a half blocks away). There was some sort of confusion with the event at Indiana Wesleyan, and they were no longer able to participate in that event. The youth leader asked if there was anybody in the area who needed any work done.

The board member arrived back at Hope Community Center and was nearly speechless. He told the story of what God had done to provide workers at Hope. A group of three or four boys during the project stood a heavy pew on its end, somehow climbed up, and painted the fifteen- to twenty-foot-high walls. I came in the door to observe it happening, turned around, and walked out, saying, "I don't even want to know!" What a joyous time—they came to do God's work, and we needed the help doing God's work! We got a picture of everyone on the front steps. I believe there were eighteen youth members and adults. We had a grand prayer time, praising God together. Oh, how He works for the glory of His name!

The prayer times we had together at Hope Community Center continued. My personal prayer life had changed a lot, and I was trusting in the Lord. We continued to have prayer weekly with what started in our friend's home as children of God wanting to see His mighty hand work. After my mentor and I returned from Brooklyn Tabernacle, I implemented my version of the thirty-day prayers that I had learned by seeing the power of this type of prayer. My personal prayer time grew and became my favorite time with the Lord. Oh, I enjoyed corporate prayer with the other folks in the community in the parking lot, but nothing lit me up like personal time with God!

God moved in many ways and touched many lives through Hope Community Center in Marion. One of the unique ways God worked was through a neighborhood daycare center. One young lady came to me asking if she could open a daycare using our building Monday through Friday. First, we prayed, asking God for His direction. We had many discussions with the board of directors, and then it quickly became evident that this young lady was serious about doing God's work in the lives of little children. She and a friend of hers headed up the effort.

It wasn't long before ten to fifteen preschoolers were involved daily at the Hope Community Day Care. I got to know the children by coming in and out on different days, and their joy was contagious, to say the least. It was a pleasure to work with the two young ladies supervising the children and taking care of the administrative tasks together with them. I think of that ministry often and thank God I had an opportunity to be a part of it.

One young man, a college-age man of God, stopped by the building one day. He asked me about the sign out front informing passersby that we had prayer every Tuesday at 1:00 p.m. and 7:00 p.m. We sat down and talked for some time. His difficult upbringing and the very difficult times that he shared in his young life brought a tear to my eye. He joined us for prayer a few times and was an active member of a local church in Marion, where he was a leader. He was thrilled to work with us in our community center, knowing it was faith-based but not church-based.

He shared a new concept with us that he called "Call to the Streets." This was a simple concept that included knocking on doors and asking people if we could pray with them over anything in their lives. Many people did not answer the door, and many times we saw someone walking down the street or mowing their grass, and we would strike up a conversation with them. It was such a simple idea that many times people would say they weren't interested, or they might just close the door. However, many times we saw people break down in tears over a loved one with cancer or a wayward teenage son or daughter. Many prayed with us, asking Jesus Christ to come into their lives.

The young leader who introduced the concept of "Call to the Streets" had started attending Indiana Wesleyan University, just a block and a half away from Hope. He was quite a leader at IWU as well, and after discussing it together, he brought several college students to the community center on Saturday mornings. They would come around 9:00 a.m. to have breakfast, engage in extensive prayer time, and then split up into groups to go calling on the streets. What a blessing that was to so many people and how honoring to God. I loved the concept, but the young people owned "Call to the Streets," and while I joined them occasionally, most of the time it was just their group.

One warm evening, I was in the community center by myself, praying at the regular time. I was alone, so I had the lights off, playing some chords on the piano and singing my heart out to the Lord. One of my favorite things about that building was that I could do that anytime. On this night, a man rode a bicycle to the side door, parked his bike, and walked into the dark sanctuary. He referred to the prayer sign outside and asked, "When is it?"

I said, "It's right now." It didn't take long to learn that this was a godly man who loved prayer. Just as we prepared to pray, our cottage prayer partners entered the dark sanctuary as well. We turned the lights on, and I introduced everyone. The gentleman who had stopped by on the bicycle advised that he would like to bring his wife and come back next week. The next week, all our wives came, and what a wonderful time we had in prayer and sharing what God was up to.

The new couple, we learned, knew of a similar program to our "Call to the Streets." We combined forces and did battle for the Lord in a very difficult area of Marion, Indiana. Many times, we would see a drug deal going down, severely mentally ill people walking the streets, or people drunk or addicted to drugs in very desperate times in their lives. God touched many lives in that area because we asked Him to. He changed many lives and led people on a course to follow Him. I know one man who was touched for eternity because of this ministry, and that was me.

One evening at a prayer meeting, our cottage prayer partners brought to our attention a house not far from the community center where some very needy people lived. They had stopped and talked with them and told them that with their permission, we would come back. We lined up the time and went back, and one adult man and two adult ladies were sitting on the porch along with a five-year-old boy. It was during the warm months, so it was very comfortable to sit outside and talk. My mentor suggested we break up into a couple of groups for prayer—one group for the men and one for the women. I wasn't sure why at the time, but I felt the Holy Spirit nudge me to break off and just pray with that five-year-old boy. We'll call him Dan.

Soon, Dan became my friend. A few times, my wife, who is a great cook, made a big dinner for the folks, and we would take it by, talk with them for a little while, pray with them, and leave them to eat. There were many dark things going on in that neighborhood and at that home. There were definite mental health issues, suspected illegal drug use, and the presence of demonic activity was notable. Several times, I went and asked permission from Dan's dad—we'll call him Ted—to take Dan out to eat or go to the nearby park. Ted was suspicious to the point of paranoia and wasn't sure whether to trust me or not.

My wife and I took Dan to the park a few times with our toy poodle. He was visibly underfed, and many times when we picked him up, he didn't have a shirt on and sometimes not even pants. Each time we took him to a fast-food place, we would go in and eat or get something and go to the park. Whenever we fed him, he would scarf down the food without a breath. It made me so sad; I would try to remind him to take his time as we didn't have to hurry.

One evening, I went by (by myself this time), and one of the ladies asked me if I could pray over their house and remove demons. She went on to say that she felt demons were in the house and that the five-year-old boy had complained about being scared and seeing things during the night. I've had some training in deliverance and prayer, but the first thing I did was pray. I began to bargain with God, saying I'm not qualified to do this—I'm not a pastor, I haven't been to seminary. I remember the Holy Spirit coming over me and telling me that He wasn't interested in excuses, but that He would provide the power; I should just pray to Him and trust Him.

"I didn't ask you if you went to seminary or where you graduated. I asked you to serve Me."

After a few minutes, I told her that I would. With the little boy's permission, I took his hand and cried out to God on his behalf. I taught him that anytime he's afraid at night or any other time, he can pray to God himself, and God will hear him. I asked the lady if I could enter the house, walk around the house, and walk around the borders of the property while praying. As I started into the house, I asked the little boy to stay on the porch with his mom and pray.

As uncertain as I was about my ability, the power of the Holy Spirit came over me. The evil forces in the house and around the house and property were palpable. I did not hurry and spent quite a lot of time walking along the perimeter of the house and through each room. As I came back to the front porch, the boy's dad arrived home. The lady sitting on the porch called the man out in front of me regarding using his phone for pornographic purposes. As comfortably and as calmly as I could, I explained to him that I would not ask, but if he was using technology for that purpose, he was reinviting demons back into the house.

Not long after this, as I went over to take Dan out to eat, his father advised me that he didn't trust me anymore and banned me from ever returning to see Dan. I was so crushed by this news that I can't explain it. I turned up the prayers for the whole group and continued to pray against Satan and his demons, crying out to God for healing for that household. One day, I was driving by their house and started praying. My heart was so heavy I began to cry and had to pull over and park. God really did some work on my heart that day as I cried out to Him. I remember the Holy Spirit, in that calm voice that I've come to learn, asking me, "How many little boys do you suppose there are in a similar situation in Marion? In Indiana? In the world?"

Then the Holy Spirit reminded me, "That boy does not need you. He needs Jesus Christ." So, I cried some more and went on my way. I would never see that little boy, Dan, again, but I prayed for him often and thanked God for the lessons He taught me. In this ministry, sometimes I would lose focus and think that somebody needed me. The truth is, I have nothing to offer anyone, but Jesus Christ has all the saving power, power over demons, healing, and He is everything that anybody needs.

Another of my favorite stories of what God has done involves a man we will call Mark. He lived across the street from the Hope Community Center. Anytime the weather was nice, he would sit on the front porch, watching traffic and waving to me as I came and went often at the community center. He saw us praying many times in the parking lot, and I invited him to join us. He did join us but never prayed, although it was obvious he enjoyed being with us.

One day, I talked with him privately and asked if he was comfortable praying with the group, as he had gotten to know us over the time he had come. He said he wasn't sure, so he and I prayed together a few times. I just reminded Mark that he didn't have to be fancy. "Just keep it simple," I would tell him. "Like me—I'm a simple man, you're a simple man, and it's okay because Jesus loves simple men." As time went on, sometimes he would pray with us, and sometimes he wouldn't, but he was always there.

I would see him walking around town, and I knew that he did not have a vehicle or drive, so I asked him one day if he drove. We became close, and sometimes I would drive him to get his check, go to the bank, or the grocery store. Many times, he would walk, but other times I would take him, sometimes to the dentist or the doctor's office. Often, I'd pick him up, go to the coffee shop, grab a cup, and sit in the car and pray. What a blessing it was to see and hear his prayer life mature.

One day, I saw him sitting on the porch. I'm not sure why, but I stopped, walked up to the porch, and started talking to him. I glanced down and saw his shoes were torn and falling off his feet. I asked him what size his shoes were, and he responded that he didn't know. I took off my left shoe and slid it over in front of him. "Try that on," I said. He looked up at me and said, "That's perfect!"

So I took off my right shoe and slid it over in front of him in the same manner. He said, "What's this?"

I simply said, "What good will one shoe do you?"

We both smiled, and he celebrated his new pair of shoes. He said, "What are you going to do now that you don't have shoes?"

I said, "Mark, I'm cleaning the carpets in the community center today. I had to take them off anyway. Please, enjoy them!"

Please don't think I'm some kind of remarkable man because I gave him my shoes. The truth is, they were very nice and very new shoes. But what you need to understand is that as a runner at that time, they were very expensive shoes, and I loved them very much—I had barely worn them. So, truth be told, when I went up on his porch, my brain was going in directions such as, "I'll take him to the store and buy him a pair of shoes," or "I'll go home and get a pair of my shoes that aren't as nice and come back and give those to him, as they would fit better with his clothing than these nice new ones."

The Holy Spirit, in that same still, small voice, I can imagine Him saying, "Stan, *seriously?*"

So again, this is about what God did completely, not anything I've done. It's one of those stories where we're going to try to outgive God, right?

Some weeks passed, and I had forgotten all about the shoe story. I was going to the community center right across from Mark's house, and as I looked across the street, I thought, *What is he doing?* He was smiling from ear to ear and pointing down at his new shoes. He was so proud of those shoes. Thank You, God, for another very valuable lesson for me!

Mark shared with me that he had a gambling problem (addiction). He would go to the Indianapolis area, and at that time, he was driving. One weekend, he went to Indy to gamble, and he spent all that he had so that he didn't even have gas money to get home. He was arrested, and he didn't know all the charges, and he didn't need to. Visiting the facility was nearly impossible, but I prayed for him for a while. I was able to keep up with his story through a friend of Mark's. He had a long sentence to serve in another county, and when he was about to be released, he found out that he had other charges pending in the county where he lived.

It was many months of incarceration, nearly a year, and I was praying that God would move in his life and that he would continue to pray with us and serve the Lord with us upon his return. Finally, he got out of jail and immediately returned to prayer time with us and came to church, sitting with my wife and me. Soon, he volunteered to cut the grass, trim, and shovel snow at the church, and what a blessing it was to see God move in this man's life.

One day, Mark asked me to drive him to the grocery store and the bank. Upon leaving the bank, we drove right past a bingo hall. I said to Mark, "Hey, man, want me to drop you off at the bingo hall? It opens in just a little bit."

He smiled and said, "No thanks, Stan. Jesus has delivered me from all that!" What a blessing to hear those words come from his mouth. Of course, I would not have taken him there anyway, and I'm not sure why I asked him, but I remember fighting back the tears (unsuccessfully) and thanking God for the friendship of this lover of Jesus Christ!

A year and a half or two years later, as the honeymoon period had worn off for the community center, I received a phone call from a sweet lady who asked an interesting question. First, she explained that she and her husband were members of a new local church, but they didn't have a building to meet in. She had left a message on my phone, and when I called her back, her husband answered. We talked for a while—a kind man—and he invited us to meet with that church body and gave us the location.

My wife and I went, and though it was very different from our usual way of worship, the people there were clearly followers of Jesus Christ. We talked with them for a while and set up a meeting for them to come and look around our community center. Three men who were on the board of the Anglican Church of the Ascension entered the building, and the Holy Spirit led from the start, as I felt compelled to ask a specific question (as I had absolutely no idea what the beliefs were in this denomination).

As the three introduced themselves, I turned to the pastor and asked, "How do I know I'm saved and I'm going to heaven?"

I didn't know this gentleman at all but came to learn early on that he was highly intelligent. He explained in detail the plan of salvation and eternal security in terms I could barely understand. As you have read, I'm a simple man. He is not. Since I knew their position on salvation, I turned to the man and said, "Let's take a tour." We toured, and very soon carved out an agreement with our board and theirs as to the terms of the purchase of the building on contract.

The story is very long, as our community center was not a church, but God led this congregation to have a place to call their own. Several months went by, and I would be retiring shortly, and my wife was not far behind. We felt the Lord calling us to move back to Kokomo to help take care of some elderly family members. The board of Hope Community Center had started to talk about what they were going to do with the community center in that time frame. The Holy Spirit led, and the Anglican Church of the Ascension made known their intent to make a final payment to complete the purchase of the building.

For many months, my wife and I had been going to the church since we were there all week anyway, and we were all lovers of Jesus— it was a great fit. From the birth of Hope Community Center, I had continually prayed that God would help this ministry survive and thrive after we left. Last Sunday, we attended church, and as the congregation was singing, I counted sixty-one people in attendance.

I sighed and thanked God and reminded Him of my prayer request. He smiled at us that day, and it was as if He asked, "Did I answer your prayer request alright, Stan?"

The boards met, and the two organizations agreed to set up a fundraiser to pay off the building before we moved to Kokomo. I won't go into the specifics, but many small gifts were given, and many large gifts were given, and the building was completely paid off. It's just like God to answer above all that we could ever ask or think.

God surely blessed us many times over with the friendships that He built through Hope Community Center and the Anglican Church of the Ascension. A dear couple, whom we came to love, were members of the board at the Anglican church and have been amazing. We have kept in contact over the years, and many prayer requests have been shared and answered between the four of us. God knows how to love us, cherish us, and show us continually how trustworthy He is. Since our mission in Marion and our move away, this couple moved farther away in a different direction. God has answered our prayers many times that we shared with our friends. God also used us to help them with prayers over the miles and time, all for the glory of His name.

When God loves us so much that He helps us identify changes that need to be made in our lives, there is pain involved. One morning, when I was feeling particularly holy, the Holy Spirit decided to deal with my pride. Not through an audible voice, but the Holy Spirit sent the message that I was to sit down and listen to Him. I had a list of things I was going to do *for the Lord*, but He wanted to change my plans for the day. I really took a spanking, but today I'm glad I did. I've been heard to say in the past that one way I recognize God working in my life is that it might involve something I don't want to do. So that morning, I sat down and listened.

The Holy Spirit spoke to me and asked me to name someone I did not like. I thought, *Wow, this is going to be easy. Do You want more than one?* The Holy Spirit replied that He wanted me to name just one. So I did. I said, "That was easy enough. Now can I start my day?"

We had a little laugh, and He said, "Not so fast."

Next, the Holy Spirit wanted me to state what it was about this person that I did not like. So my question was, "Just one thing, or should I list numerous things?"

His reply was, "As many as you can think of."

The first five or six things were easy; numbers 7 and 8 took a little more thought. My response was, "Now can I start my day and do all these good deeds I had in mind?"

Again, He said, "Not so fast."

You see, after naming the first five or six items that I did not like about this individual, I was actually naming things about myself that needed to be fixed. My heart started to soften. Now I was really ready to leave and go about my day, but the Holy Spirit grabbed me and said, *Now I want you to think about this person you said you didn't like. I want you to pray a blessing on this person—not just for them to have a blessed day, but I mean asking God to bless them deeply in everything that they do.* I started what turned out to be a long prayer. Tears started to flow, my heart softened, and by the end of the prayer, I was thanking God for how He changed me that day.

You see, it was not the target of my dislike who needed to change that day—though in my prayer, I asked God to speak with him and help him change what God said needed changing—but it was me who needed to change. I thank God that He loved me enough to break my heart and change me for the glory of His name.

In June of 2021, we received a phone call regarding the death of a family member. This death was not an accident or a fall, but a murder, burglary, criminal confinement, and several other crimes. The victim was a relative of mine by marriage, but it still hit me very hard, to say the least. I don't plan to share the gruesome details of these crimes, but what your imagination can conjure is not as bad as the truth in this case. My intent here is to share how God changed my life in the process of trying to cope with all of this.

Of course, the news media reported many details about the crimes and the man who perpetrated them. Being a retired police officer and a retired nurse, I was more than casually aware of criminal law, physical injuries, and mental health issues, as mental health was my specialty in the nursing field and arguably in police work. The more I learned, the more I didn't want to know. This paradox caused some mental health issues in me. Of course, with the media stories, I was aware of the perpetrator's name, the details of the crimes, and the trial proceedings.

I began to pray for the suspect, the judge, the prosecutor, the defense attorney, and the jail staff where the defendant was held. Over the course of a year, I kept up with the case, prayed, and wrote letters to the people listed above in the court system, as well as to the defendant. My letters thanked those involved in the legal process for their work, inquired about the availability of visitation and phone calls, and asked the defendant if he would meet with me. The only response I received was from the jail commander, explaining the process. The defendant would not or could not respond to my letter. I continued to pray regularly for the staff overseeing the case and for the defendant.

I was a little confused about how to pray. Knowing the victim, the torture, and the details, I found myself praying to the God of justice that this man's life would be taken from him and that he would be cast into hell. I'm not proud of this truth, but you can imagine the impact this event had on my life. There were other times when I prayed for the defendant to receive Christ, followed by asking God to help my unbelief. After about a year of following and praying, the Holy Spirit sat me down for another lesson. The lesson was the same as when the Holy Spirit asked me to name an individual I did not like.

That lesson had stuck well from before, and as I recognized what was going on, the tears came. As I prayed and asked God to forgive me, it became real that I desperately needed Him to overcome my pride and the strongholds I tend to keep in my life. When I think about this, I thank God for doing His work in me, and I pray that the perpetrator will turn to Christ and be forgiven just like me. In a men's prayer group that I attend regularly, a gentleman shared how he used to minister to people in a nearby prison. I worked in that prison as an RN, and it happens to be the prison that houses the offender in the above-described case. I'm involved in several ministries now, but who knows—if the Holy Spirit leads, maybe I'll get a chance to speak with him and pray with him. Oh, for the glory of His name.

In November 2021, deer season had arrived. We had a favorite hunting spot that had a story all its own. It belonged to my brother. He, two of my sons, and I went there on opening day each year. This particular year, I had announced it would be my last. I shared with the boys that I would still come out for the company when I thought it was time to step down. For many years, I had prayed for successful hunts for my sons and my brother. This year was different. While driving in the dark and praying, thanking God for the farm and the experiences of hunting there, a tear came to my eye. I had shot many deer over the years and enjoyed the meat, but I had never had the opportunity to harvest the big buck. In the car, I prayed, and I believed that He would be faithful and answer.

We always tried to go out well before sunrise, and this time was no different. There were trails to our deer stands, and, in some way, I got off the trail. The area was not so large that one could get lost. I was aggravated at first, but just after hunting light, I found my way. As I climbed up onto my stand and got situated, I decided to lay my head back and take a nap. Getting into my comfortable position, I decided to open my eyes for just a moment. I'm not even sure why. As I opened my eyes, a blur went across the tree line to the west of me. It went so fast that I wasn't sure what it was. If you've ever hunted, you know deer sprinting looks about ten blocks long and very narrow. If you've ever seen the cartoon *The Pink Panther*, it looked like the Roadrunner.

I didn't see anything for a couple of minutes, then I heard the familiar crunching through the corn cobs and the roughage. Three deer came in from the north, wandered around within range for just a few seconds, then headed northeast. That part of the area is thick with brush and made seeing them impossible. As I sat in my stand patiently, I remembered thinking I'd either see them again or another deer. And in just a few minutes, the threesome came back into my shooting zone.

It's okay if you think I'm crazy, but I sensed the Holy Spirit asking me which one I wanted. Of the three, there was a small buck, a doe (known as bait), and a big buck. I whispered, *I'll take the big buck.* Almost immediately, the big buck walked right toward my stand. I was so excited, knowing where the blessing was coming from, and confident that I would have a good shot. I did have a successful shot, and what a celebration followed. I've seen much larger bucks harvested from the area by my brother, who is a hunter. I've never seen a larger buck the times I'm out there. I have many memories of how God blessed us with the farm, the campfires, the hunting, and, most of all, the memory of my big buck, whose head now hangs on my wall in the office. Thanks be to God.

Prior to our move to Kokomo, Rhonda and I were contacted by a pastor in Kokomo who taught us about dinner church. The concept was very interesting to us both, so we attended a training course on the subject. We had already ministered to several veterans at an apartment complex on the south side of Marion. We had met with different veterans individually and in groups for Bible study, prayer time, and addiction support groups. We really enjoyed the training for dinner church and agreed with the administration of the apartment complex that it would be a great ministry for the veterans.

Once per month, on a Saturday, we would get together to have a meal, prepared without cost by volunteers from the Hope Community Center and a couple of churches. Following the meal, we would have a fifteen- or twenty-minute devotional, talking about Jesus and some of His miracles. The volunteers were careful to sit at separate tables so veterans could meet new Jesus lovers and have someone to hear their prayer requests and pray with them. This was one of my favorite ministries while at the Hope Community Center.

One of my favorite stories, a true *God thing*, involved a veteran who was living at the apartment complex and passed away. He had no family and no minister to lead a memorial service for him. I was approached by an administrator of the apartment complex and asked if I would do the memorial service. It was another situation where I doubted my abilities, as I had not been to seminary or had formal training as a pastor. As with other situations, the Holy Spirit said, "Stan, I did not ask you where you went to school. Just go." After praying and asking God to have His way, I found that it was not that difficult. By the day of the service, a distant relative had heard of the veteran's passing and learned of the memorial service, and she decided to attend. It was a great touch from heaven that she came. We sang a few songs; I spoke briefly about the plan of salvation, prayed, and allowed attendees to comment on the veteran's life. There weren't many comments, as not many knew very much about the veteran. Several comments were heard after the service about how they were blessed by the service. Praise be to God!

Rhonda and I learned of a place to serve the Lord in Kokomo. It is a wonderful place to gather with people of faith, put together cards with the plan of salvation, and include a cross. The plan is to mail these cards to every mailbox in the United States of America. While we were living in Marion, we would come intermittently, prepare crosses and cards for mailing, and meet many new friends. Having completed our mission in Marion and having parents in Kokomo who needed a little support, we headed for Kokomo.

Upon getting settled in Kokomo and moving to a nice independent living facility, the Lord opened some new opportunities to serve Him and make many friends. Many people at the assisted living facility had physical needs that were met by the facility. It wasn't long before we found ourselves praying with many of them at their request. Someone suggested we have a Bible study where we could meet, learn, and pray together. It wasn't long before Rhonda began leading a Bible study every evening before dinner. It was a rather large undertaking, so I assisted Rhonda in this endeavor. What a blessing it was for us to serve in this manner. Several of the men would come and talk with me, and the ladies with Rhonda. Many questions would arise during difficult times in life about salvation and how one can know they are saved. It was a wonderful time to share what the Lord has done for us with needy people when their hearts are ripe for the Lord. We are so thankful for the opportunity to serve Him in several *mission fields*.

One Thursday morning, when Rhonda and I were serving at Cross America, a friend from many years ago came to our table and invited me to the men's Bible study and prayer time held at Cross America each Thursday morning. He explained that the church he attends hosts the Bible study and that he loves it. The next Thursday, Rhonda came with me and folded cards with crosses while I attended the men's Bible study. I felt welcome from the time I arrived, to say the least. Soon, some very close relationships formed, and I felt right at home. Pastor Brian Hughes led the group of Jesus lovers, and I sensed the Holy Spirit's presence at the Bible study for a year and a half.

I love the name of the men's group. It is called Men of the House. Several weeks after attending, Pastor Brian asked me if I would lead the group the next week, as he had another commitment. I said I would be delighted to, so I did. He asked me to lead the group on a few other occasions, and after a few times of leading, he asked me to pray about leading Men of the House each week. I am richly blessed by the Lord to have a great group of Jesus lovers who also love each other and minister to one another.

I believe it was the first time I attended Men of the House that the pastor announced an event called Kokomo Table. As he explained the details, I learned it was the exact same program that Rhonda and I had been involved with in Marion. It was called Dinner Church. It was to be held on the fourth Wednesday evening of each month. We stayed after to talk to the pastor about the program, excited to share that we love the Dinner Church concept. Further conversation revealed that it was the same pastor and congregation who had pro-vided the training for Dinner Church. The pastor invited Rhonda and me to come, and we've been involved ever since, leading the conversation after the devotional and prayer time.

My friend from childhood invited us along to Reach Church. We had already been to two of the church's events and loved attend-ing, where we found a very diverse congregation of people who were excited about what God was doing in north Kokomo. Another close friend of many years was at Cross America one morning, and we had a long conversation and got caught up. I invited him to our men's group (Men of the House), and he came. He said he really liked it and has been attending ever since. It's great to see him each week and to talk about our love for the Lord and what He is doing in our churches and our families. He and I attended a training seminar about podcasting. We've had many conversations about starting a podcast with a particular focus. I'm excited to see what the Lord is doing in this regard, as we both love the Lord and want more glory in His name.

Back in the early days of my Christian walk, a few men had a lot to do with shaping my core beliefs. I'm so thankful for them, as I had a good foundation of who God is and who I was in Him. In my mid-fifties, I felt stuck in the mud and frustrated with where I was spiritually. I started crying out to the Lord in prayer, and He healed me and continues to heal me. He pointed out to me some areas in my life that needed to change for me to become closer to Him. As we know, with change comes pain many times. I had become a self-ish man and was no longer satisfied with my relationship with the Lord. Satan had some strongholds in my life and continued to lie to me, and I continued to get less satisfied and emptier. I found that I couldn't find my way out of these strongholds on my own. By truly crying out to God and bearing my soul to Him, He has given and continues to give me victory over sin.

You see, the living God wants the same relationship with me that I want with Him. He is more than capable and ready to draw me closer and closer to Him, and what a beautiful thing that is. I have many friends who are believers, encouragers, and accountability partners who have been very helpful in my walk. I strongly desire these men in my life, and I need them as well. What I am finding, however, is that my favorite times include my personal prayer time and studying God's Word. I'm enjoying much more sharing Jesus Christ with others who desperately need Him just like me.

When I was stuck in my old way of black-and-white thinking, I was more interested in how to convince people to believe about God what I believed, and I would engage in arguments with that goal in mind. Now I'm asking God to show me His beautiful face and teach me more about His word. How freeing that is, and life is becoming a living color to me. The freedom given to me by the Lord Jesus Christ gives me hope.

In late 2018, I made a little plaque that went over my recliner for a year. The plaque said, "Freedom 2019." I had been crying out to

God, and I wanted to be free. I knew that if I wanted true freedom, the kind that God wants for me to have, it probably would not be an overnight change and it would require listening to God and learning how to get there. Well, 2019 has come and gone, and God has taught me much about freedom. I would say that I am now free and that it is an ongoing process.

I remember back when I was in bondage, speaking with one of my mentors about the fact that I just couldn't talk to people about Jesus and what He's done for me. And his perfect answer came in the form of a question: *Has Jesus Christ ever done anything for you?* In giving me this freedom, it has become much easier to share with others what Jesus Christ has done for me. You see, simply put, it is *not* all about me, but it *is* all about Him. God has changed me so much that now when I have a discussion with someone on a spiritual matter, I'm relaxed and don't feel pressured to convince them that I'm right. Many times, I'll share how God has changed me over time and how freeing that has been.

When I was not free, many times I would just call on God when I wanted something. Now during my prayer time, I'll share with Him my concerns or concerns for others. Many times, when I'm crying out to God for others who ask me to pray for them for wisdom or healing, I will ask God to include me and my needs. He has changed me into a guy who likes to just check in now. My Abba Father has turned into my friend who sticks closer than a brother. I don't just say a quick prayer at mealtimes, but I like to talk with Him about what's going on in my life while I'm taking a walk or riding my bicycle through town. I love it that He gives me what I need and not just what I want, though many times when He's giving me what I need, it comes with pain.

One of my favorite scriptures has become Romans 15:13. It says,

> Now the God of hope fill you with all joy
> and peace in believing, that ye may abound in
> hope, through the power of the Holy Ghost.

Many times, we will read that verse at the end of our prayer time at Men of the House Bible study. It is so comforting to have true hope. Especially these days, it's hard for me to put hope in anything or in anybody else but Jesus Christ.

In putting these thoughts and ideas together for this work, the Holy Spirit many times brought me new things I wanted to share. This morning in Sunday school, I shared in response to the question that Rhonda put on the table: When was it that God changed your life, and how did that impact your life? My answer was that He changed my life when He taught me I could not earn my salvation. How it changed my life was in every way. As I continued to grapple with that question, I began to understand how much Jesus Christ in me gives me hope, encouragement, and strength. Meeting with fellow believers and discussing such questions is very valuable to me.

One of the attendees of this morning's Sunday school class was the reason we began attending Reach Church. He and I had a close relationship in grade school, Little League baseball, and in high school. I have always loved him and appreciated his sense of humor. Upon graduation from high school, we went for many years without seeing each other. It's so refreshing each week when I see him. We share stories about the past, and I love to hear the stories where Jesus has touched his life, and I love telling the ones where He's touched mine. He shared with me that he has a son who has struggled with some things that I've struggled with as well. He asked if I would mind meeting with his son and praying with him. We met each week for over a year, and I've come to love his son as well and watched the Lord's work in his life. I watched the Lord work in my life as well.

On May 10, 2024, The Weather Channel that Rhonda and I watch shared that sometime during the night, the Northern Lights would appear. I don't know a lot about how science works, but they had a designated time for the best viewing and designated places throughout the country where one might witness God's creation. We were winding down our day and thought we'd go ahead and head to bed. We got to talking, and I believe we agreed it was past the ideal time to witness the Northern Lights. We decided to put our slippers back on and take a walk outside.

Construction was going on at the north end of the property where we stay (Waterford Place), so we walked off to the darker portion where we could get a good look at the sky. We walked into that darkened area holding hands, as we had many times before. I let go of her hand, and she continued to walk as I stayed put. She continued a couple of hundred yards and then stopped. I remember thinking for a moment that we were outside the timeline and potentially the ideal area where we could see the Northern Lights.

As I looked up into the heavens, I asked God to show me a part of who He is. I thanked Him for the beauty I had already beheld on our little walk. Continuing to worship Him and give Him thanks, the Northern Lights appeared, and it was a mighty wave from the hand of God that I received as the gift He intended it to be. We were both in awe of what God had shown us. As I approached her and held her hand again, we discussed what had just happened. She was praying for God to show us, as I was praying for God to show us, and He did! Some would say it was going to happen anyway and it was just a coincidence. Anyone who would say that doesn't know my God. I remember a few tears being shed that night and many prayers of thanksgiving for how the Creator of the heavens and the earth loves me that much.

Speaking with a friend yesterday, we spoke about how God is still writing my story. I think I've completed it, and then there's more. In these stories, there are several people who have accepted Christ into their lives. The Lord continues to teach me that it's not my works but my heart, which I've tried to dedicate to Him, that makes all the difference.

One man—we will call him Gary—I have had several conversations with him regarding the question of how I can know I'm saved. As I gave him the truth, I wondered if there was something he wouldn't give up or was unwilling to do. Gary was right where I've been, but he doesn't know where I am. And I'm not where I am due to anything other than the blood of Jesus Christ. It disturbs me that so many churches today have this candy-coated Christianity, where if you accept Jesus Christ, your problems are over. I have found the opposite to be true.

One of my mentors, after several discussions with him, pointed me in a direction that was very clear to me at the time, and I'll never forget. He explained that if you're ready to become a Christian, you need to be ready to die. Die to self, sin, and die with Jesus Christ so that you may be risen with Him on that day. I encourage Gary and others I speak with that the journey to Jesus is different for everyone. The way to salvation is the same, but the route taken can be very different. It's important to note that Jesus Christ and the Holy Spirit will help us to die to self and sin. And it's not about a bunch of actions, such as "I must stop smoking or stop drinking or stop doing this or that" or "Start doing this and that." Jesus Christ is the way, the truth, and the life, and no one comes to the Father except by Him.

A couple of scripture verses that have been helpful to me include John 14:23:

> If a man loves me, he will keep my words.

As God continues to mature me in the faith, I've gone from a false feeling of salvation by works to giving Him my whole heart. This concept shows up in many actions, such as worship, scripture reading, and prayer. But it's not the acts; it's the faith that brings the habitual acts of good works. James 2:14–20: *It takes both faith and works.*

1 John 1:3–4 says:

> That which we have seen and heard declare
> we unto you that you may also have fellowship
> with us and truly our fellowship is with the Father
> and with his Son Jesus Christ and these things
> write we into you that your joy may be full.

Think about that: your joy may be full. This brings up some different ideas in my mind over the years about what joy is and what joy is not.

I've shared many times about a motorcycle crash that I had and about a beatdown by an angry mob. Joy is having Jesus Christ in my life, and no matter what happens, the situation is in His hands. This is joy. Joy is not something good that happens to me that brings about pleasure or attention of some sort. Joy is hearing His still, small voice in the middle of a disaster. Joy used to be some other things to me, but now it is watching God's hand work every day, sometimes in small ways and sometimes in big ways, but always in ways that show His power and grace. Joy is watching someone else come to Christ after sharing what He's done for me and explaining that I'm no more special or less special than anybody else. It's Jesus Christ that makes all the difference.

Five weeks ago, I lost my wallet while on a bicycle ride downtown. First, we prayed, my wife and I, because we knew the importance of all the contents of my wallet. It's frustrating going through the process of replacing all the insurance cards, driver's license, etc. I was sure the Lord would show us where I lost it, so I drove a few miles retracing my steps from the bike ride to no avail. I had a small amount of cash in my wallet, and while it wasn't very significant that it was gone, it was frustrating nonetheless.

Today during my devotion time, my phone rang. It was an unfamiliar number, and I'm still not sure why I answered, but a kind voice on the other end asked, "Is this Mr. Ridlen?"

Upon identifying myself, the kind young lady stated, "I have your wallet."

She gave me the address of the rehab facility where she was working, and I thanked her and told her I'd be right there. As I entered and she was looking for me, she handed me the wallet, smiled, and said, "Have a good day."

I said, "Wait a minute—who turned it in? Where did they find it?"

She said, "I don't know his name, sir. He was obviously homeless and just walked in, handed me the wallet, and said, 'I found this.'"

As I opened the wallet, the small amount of cash was still there. There was also another piece of identification that meant a lot to me, and it remained in the wallet. As I reentered the vehicle with my wife, she had questions like those above, and maybe a few others. I had no answers. A discussion ensued about how good God is. He is good all the time, with the big things and the small things. Even in this small thing, my joy is full because in my life I know who's driving. And I know who's not.

Our family utilizes a sense of humor that I have really come to love. A few years ago, Mom had to have open-heart surgery to replace a valve. She was at a hospital in northwest Indianapolis that was connected to Peyton Manning Hospital. As I prepared to leave that evening, Mom was still groggy. I told her, "I'm going to walk through Peyton Manning's hospital, as I've heard that occasionally he goes room to room visiting sick kids."

The next day, as I arrived to see Mom, I told her, "I ran into Mr. Manning in the hall and asked him if I could go into a room or two with him." I don't think she was buying it, but I carried my storyline out.

I said, "Mom, you wouldn't even believe it. I asked him in the hall if I could visit a patient or two with him, as I am a registered nurse." I continued the story, saying that Mr. Manning advised he would have to check with the family first in this one room we were going to visit. So as I waited in the hall, he went into the room. As he got about halfway across the room, he just turned and, with that sheepish look on his face, returned to me in the hall. I excitedly said, "What did they say?"

He said that as he was getting across the room, the young boy said, "Who's that guy with Stan?" By now, Mom was playing along, but I was having fun. We remained in the hallway for a minute, then I stepped toward the door. Mr. Manning said, "Where are you going?"

I told him, "I'm going to ask the family if it's okay if you come in to visit with them for a few minutes." We all had a good laugh, and that was that. I've told that story a few times since, and it's always good for a laugh or two. There are so many serious things in life that bring us down at times, but it's good to utilize humor when we can.

There are many more stories where I've had a front seat to appreciate what God is doing and has done. Many of them have touched my life through successes in other people's lives as well as my own. I have really come to appreciate the power of my Lord and

Savior as I ask Him for help to overcome an addiction, battling sins such as gossip, and God's showing up with His power to overcome my fears and trials. He is so faithful in helping me as I continue to try to ask God for what He already wants.

God came to seek and to save us and for us to be free from sin and bondage. It only makes sense that He is more than pleased to help us be free and remain that way. I'm so thankful for the stories I've shared and many more that are still being written. It is in sharing with others that the Great Commission can be advanced. He continues to bless me and free me.

I would like to end this work with one of my favorite passages of Scripture, Isaiah 61:1–3:

> The spirit of the Lord God is upon me because the Lord hath anointed me to preach good tidings unto the meek; he has sent me to bind up the broken hearted to proclaim liberty to the captives and the opening of the prison to them that are bound; to proclaim the acceptable year of the Lord and the day of vengeance of our God to comfort all that mourn to appoint unto them that mourn and Zion to given to them beauty for ashes the oil of joy for mourning the garment of praise for the spirit of heaviness that they might be called trees of righteousness the planting of the Lord that he might be glorified.